Advance praise for *Military Life: The Insider's Guide*...

"I highly recommend this book for anyone who wants a realistic, balanced, and up-to-date picture of life in the American military. It's a truly impressive accomplishment: a gold mine of information for young people considering service in the military, active-duty personnel, and the inquiring citizen."

> —*Gene R. La Rocque*
> *Rear Admiral, USN (Ret.)*
> *Director, Center for Defense*
> *Information*

"This is a first. Never before has the story of military service, rights, and duties been told by someone other than officialdom. This book truly serves."

> —*Studs Terkel*
> *Author,* The Good War: An Oral History of
> World War II

"Anyone thinking of joining one of the military services should read *Military Life.*"

> —*John B. Kidd*
> *Major General, US Air Force (Ret.)*

"I think that any young person who is considering a military career will benefit from reading this book. Mr. Ensign pulls no punches in describing all facets of military life."

> —*Thomas J. Gumbleton*
> *Auxiliary Bishop of Detroit*

"Factual, unbiased, and complete ... Any student who is contemplating entrance to military service should have this book's contents made available for consideration."

> —*James B. Burkholder*
> *Colonel, US Army (Ret.)*

"I commend the author for fulfilling the need for a common-sense guide for younger Americans who are considering joining the US armed forces. The strength and appeal of this book derive from its independent, objective viewpoint. This approach will bring useful balance to the rosy impressions left by TV 'bites' and the recruiter's story.

"This book nicely describes the timeless verities of life in the military. It's a well-crafted product that will fulfill a clear and present need."

> —*William C. Mannix*
> *Colonel, US Air Force (Ret.)*

MILITARY LIFE
THE INSIDER'S GUIDE

Tod Ensign, Esq.

New York London Toronto Sydney Tokyo Singapore

Copyright © 1990 by Alternatives to Militarism, Inc.

 A R C O

9396584

Simon & Schuster, Inc.
15 Columbus Circle
New York, NY 10023

An Arco Book
Published by Prentice Hall

Prentice Hall and colophons are
registered trademarks of Simon & Schuster, Inc.

Manufactured in the United States of America

2   3   4   5   6   7   8   9   10

Library of Congress Cataloging-in-Publication Data

Ensign, Tod.   Military life : the insider's guide / Tod Ensign. — 1st
Prentice Hall ed.
     p.   cm.
   Includes bibliographical references.
   ISBN 0-13-582529-6
   1. United States—Armed Forces—Handbooks, manuals, etc.
2. United States—Armed Forces—Military life—Handbooks, manuals,
etc.   I. Title.
U113.E57   1990   90-1176
355′.00973--dc20   CIP

CONTENTS

Dedication

For Francine

Acknowledgements

Tricia Critchfield, my assistant, made a large contribution to this Guide, helping with both research and the preparation of the manuscript. My colleague, Louis Font, Esq., shared his extensive knowledge of many military legal issues with me.

A book such as this depends, to borrow Tennessee Williams' phrase, on the "kindness of strangers." In this category are the military public affairs officers around the world who, with few exceptions, eagerly assisted me with this work.

I want to extend a special thanks to some of the many low-ranking "grunts" who also helped bring this guide to life. Among these fine people are: Joe Wojak, Craig Higgins, Jerry Caldwell, John Childs, Roy Beauchamp, Mark Lane, Glenn Baker, Dave Allen, Orlando Green, Darcy Ross, and John Brisbois.

I also want to thank Rob Hager, Esq., Kathy and Wayland Heim, Hal Harris, Helen Michalowski, Mrs. Sidney Hickey, Michael Mauer, Esq., and Dave Freedman for their help.

Chapter 1

Recruitment

The military is our country's largest employer, with over 4 million Americans currently on its payroll. Over 2 million of these service members are on active duty, with over 500,000 of them stationed outside the continental United States at any given time. Although it's hard to generalize about any institution this large, there are certain experiences that are common to most GI's. This book aims to provide you with an inside look at what it's really like to be a part of today's peacetime military. Please realize, however, that no two military experiences will ever be the same. There will always be some variation, depending on the type of military unit in which you serve.

MYTHS VERSUS REALITY

Thousands of books, movies, and television programs have used the American military as the subject of their stories. By the time the average teenager reaches recruiting age, he* probably will have read some of these books and watched hundreds of television shows and movies with military themes.

However, most of these books, television shows, and movies focus on only one aspect of military life—warfare. Although combat scenes may be entertaining (at least for the spectator), they don't provide a portrait of life in today's peacetime military. The U.S. military has undergone considerable changes since the Vietnam War and the draft ended.

It is often difficult for a young person to get a balanced picture of military life today. Recruiters have many brochures and pam-

---

*To save space, I have chosen to use only the masculine reference, instead of writing out "he/she" or "men/women" every time. This is not intended, in any way, to disparage or overlook the substantial contributions women have made (and will make) to our military.

phlets that present the positive aspects of service. This book, however, will attempt to provide a more objective view. The armed services, like any large organization, have their good and bad points, with some "grey areas" as well.

Each year, about 250,000 new recruits are sworn into active duty. Many enlist because they hope to earn college-assistance funds or because they want vocational-skills training. Others join in search of adventure, travel, and excitement. Often, several of these factors contribute to one's decision to enlist.

The "all volunteer" military has undergone significant change in recent years. Listed below are some common misconceptions.

MYTH: GI's live in bunk-house-style barracks, eat indigestible food in dingy chowhalls, and venture off base mainly on Saturday nights when they drink and brawl in base-town saloons.

REALITY: The majority of enlisted people today are married. They live with their spouses and children in houses or apartments both on and off base. Single GI's who live on base usually occupy modern, brick, apartment-style buildings where they share semi-private quarters with one or two other GI's. An Army private today earns about $814 a month, in addition to receiving free room and board. People who don't live on base may spend as much time with civilians as they do with military personnel.

MYTH: Military people spend most of their time preparing for combat. This means firing weapons, camping in tents, marching, and playing war games.

REALITY: Today's military offers over 2,000 different jobs to enlisted people, many of which have almost no connection to warfare. GI's perform a wide range of jobs, from computer programming, to pharmacy, to court stenography. Many GI's learn job skills that later can be used for civilian employment. However, there *are* military jobs, such as firing artillery or spotting aerial bombardment, that will not be of much use when looking for a civilian job.

MYTH: Military units tend to be composed predominantly of white men, like in television shows such as "M*A*S*H."

REALITY: African-Americans, Hispanics, and women constitute the majority in many military units today. Minority GI's also tend to reenlist at higher rates than do whites. Many feel that the equal-opportunity climate in the armed forces is better than what exists on the outside.

MYTH: The military is pretty much like any other job, except that you always wear a uniform.

REALITY: The military is a separate society. It has many rules and laws that aren't found in civilian society. Military commanders have more authority over their subordinates than do civilian employers. If a GI writes a "bad" check, for example, he may be punished by his commanding officer. Military police have the authority to search a footlocker or other property in situations where civilian police could not.

If you are seriously considering enlistment, you will want to compare what the recruiters are offering with civilian alternatives. One of the military's best selling points is that it provides GI's with decent pay, room and board, and other benefits while it teaches them a skill. Even if you don't receive training that you can later apply to a civilian job, you are still piling up college-assistance money that can total more than $20,000 for just one 3-year hitch. Also, some people find that the structure and discipline of military life helps to straighten them out and teach them good work habits.

Quick Quiz: Are You Suited for Military Life?

Take a few minutes to answer the following nine questions as honestly as you can.

1. Can you tolerate strenuous physical activity?

    ☐ Yes   ☐ No

2. Any organization with over 4 million employees is going to operate with complicated rules and layers of bureaucracy. Will you be comfortable being a small cog in a very big machine?

    ☐ Yes   ☐ No

3. Will you mind wearing the same uniform as everyone else and obeying fairly strict rules of conduct and appearance?

   ☐ Yes   ☐ No

4. Are you willing to take annual tests that check for drug residue in your urine and for AIDS antibodies in your blood?

   ☐ Yes   ☐ No

5. In general, do you obey rules, even if you think that they're unfair, unnecessary, or just plain stupid?

   ☐ Yes   ☐ No

6. The military considers GI's to be subject to its rules 24 hours a day. Can you accept the regulation of your off-base social life?

   ☐ Yes   ☐ No

7. If something goes wrong, are you generally willing to work within "the system" rather than publicizing your complaints?

   ☐ Yes   ☐ No

8. Are you willing to be tested each year to prove that you're competent to perform your assigned job?

   ☐ Yes   ☐ No

9. Can you handle military training that teaches you how to use weapons in order to kill other human beings?

   ☐ Yes   ☐ No

If you've answered "no" to two or three questions, I would recommend that you spend some additional time talking with people on active duty before you sign an enlistment contract. If you answered "no" to most of the questions, you should give serious thought to another line of work.

Soliciting Friendly Advice

Seek out friends who are either on active duty or who just got out. Ask them a lot of questions about their experiences. You'll have to evaluate what they say in light of your own likes and dislikes. What bugs someone else might roll right past you, and vice versa. When someone expresses highly negative opinions, you should consider whether his service experiences have left him biased.

The important questions to answer are: Can you obtain the things that the military offers (job training, work experience, college aid, travel, and adventure) from some other source? Second, are your attitudes and lifestyle reasonably compatible with the way military people are expected to live? If you can answer "no" to the first question and "yes" to the second, then the armed forces may be a good place for you.

Are Your Expectations Realistic?

Young people sometimes think they can solve all of their problems by joining the military. If you enter the armed forces with poor academic skills or a history of failure in various jobs, it is unreasonable to expect to change these problems overnight. If you enlist as a way to escape problems you are having with your parents or girlfriend, you may be disappointed. A change of scene won't, by itself, straighten out complicated emotional issues like these.

Welcome to the "All-Volunteer" Military!

The last American draftee entered the Army on June 30, 1973, just before the draft was abolished. An anti-war movement by millions of Americans who opposed the Vietnam War was instrumental in ending the draft. Since then, the 2.1-million-member armed forces have been composed entirely of volunteers. The challenge of recruiting 250,000 new volunteers each year dwarfs anything in the military's past. Our entire military just before World War II was only slightly larger than today's annual recruiting quota!

Today, the Pentagon spends about $2 billion each year on recruiting. The Army alone uses almost 9,000 full-time recruiters to sign young people to enlistment contracts.

SELLING THE ARMED FORCES

No one who watches television or listens to the radio can miss the military's message to young recruiting prospects. An annual advertising budget in excess of $200 million ensures that virtually every member of the primary "target audience" (seventeen to twenty-one-year-old males) sees or hears the ads. The television ads show attractive young people doing military jobs that appear both challenging and important. One advertising executive explained the philosophy of this advertising: "The purpose of these ads isn't to make you rush out and do something. [They're] intended to make that 'something' known to you . . . and to bring it within the range of acceptable [choices]."

The ads are also designed to appeal to another audience—your parents. Another advertising executive observed, "Kids like to deny their parents' role, but our studies show that they can have a heavy influence in a matter like joining the military."

The Pentagon and its advertising agencies conduct regular opinion polls to determine what motivates young people to enlist. Recent surveys have shown that vocational opportunities and qualifying for college assistance are the strongest motives for enlistment. Your sex, race, age, and level of education all play a part in influencing whether or not you enlist. For example, pollsters have learned that about one in three young men had a favorable opinion of enlistment, compared with less than one in six for women. Black males are twice as likely as white males to think well of military service, while black females are three times as positive toward military service as white females.

Each service branch gives its advertising a particular emphasis. The Army's, for example, seeks to convey an image of a high-tech and modern institution. Its ads emphasize the attainment of personal goals; skills training, college aid, etc. In contrast, advertisements for the Marines challenge young people to aspire to become "one of the few, the proud." Little is said of the vocational benefits of serving. The Navy and Air Force ads fall somewhere in between these two. They stress both pride in serving one's country and opportunities for personal advancement.

UNIQUE ASPECTS OF MILITARY LIFE

The Chain of Command: A Key Concept

"Respect the uniform—not necessarily the person wearing it," is an expression you sometimes hear in the military. It means that you obey an order because you respect the rank of the person giving it, not necessarily the person himself. Where you stand in terms of the rank scale is very important in the military.

The Navy's Bible for new sailors, the *Bluejacket's Manual*, explains the concept: "The chain of command exists to ensure that ... there will be no doubt where you or anyone else stands in the chain." There's really nothing like this idea in civilian society, except perhaps for the discipline imposed by the police or fire departments.

If your superior officer gives you an order that you think may be improper or illegal, you are in a ticklish spot. If you obey, you may bring trouble on yourself in the future. If you refuse, however, you are almost certain to be called to account immediately. The military does provide mechanisms for questioning orders, but only within your immediate chain of command. GI's are told to register serious complaints with their unit's Inspector General (IG).

Weigh In or Way Out!

Recruits are often surprised to learn that the military has strenuous physical requirements. Everyone on active duty, regardless of their job, must pass physical qualification tests twice a year. To qualify, a soldier must be able to do a certain number of sit-ups and push-ups (scaled to their age) and complete a two-mile run in less than twenty minutes. Most GI's (whatever their rank) must participate in organized calisthenics several times a week—before, during, or after duty hours. Those who fail their semi-annual test are placed on a special exercise regimen. If they continue to fail qualification tests, they can be discharged. The same thing applies for body weight; each GI must keep it within prescribed guidelines. For those who put on extra pounds, it's "lose it or see ya later."

Points to Reflect Upon

As an institution, the military emphasizes conformity and discourages most expressions of individualism. Because many military jobs *do* require a high degree of teamwork, those who are team players are more likely to be rewarded. Presently, about one in three new recruits fails to complete his first term of enlistment. This rate has remained the same for the past ten years or so.

Whether or not to join the military is an important question that only you can answer. This is probably the first major life decision that you will make on your own. Be sure that you give it the careful thought that such an important decision deserves.

THE WORLD OF THE RECRUITER

> *"We ask our recruiters to be honest and to explain fully what life in the military really is."*
>
> —MAJ. GEN. ALLEN K. ONO,
>   FORMER CHIEF, ARMY RECRUITING

The typical military recruiter today has served six to eight years and plans to make a career of the military. The average recruiter must enlist between two and three new recruits each month, although this will vary by region and service branch. Many military people consider recruiting to be an extremely difficult and stressful job, to be avoided if possible.

Until recently, the services were able to attract all the recruits they needed. In 1989, however, the Army and the Marines failed to meet their quotas, and the Navy was forced to lower entrance requirements in order to fill its ranks. Most manpower experts blame these shortages on the fact that the pool of eligible young people is shrinking. Whatever the cause, the always-difficult job of recruiting has become even tougher.

According to the military, a total of 4,159 allegations of recruiting fraud were investigated in the 1988 fiscal year. Of those, 701 were found to be valid and 992 recruiters were disciplined—about 7 percent of the total recruiting force. A Congressional report on recruiting published in 1989 concluded that "undue pressure" on recruiters by their superiors to meet quotas was the cause of many of these abuses.

Recruiters work in a complicated quota system. The manpower needs of each branch change constantly, sometimes from one hour to the next. Recruiters must try to fit the qualifications and wishes of recruits to the training slots and job assignments available. One recruiter recently described this situation to the *Navy Times*: "You think [you are] going out there to help people who want to join the Navy. Wrong! We are tied to a system [in which] each service will recruit so many high school grads, so many upper-mental and lower-mental categories, and so many females. It's common for a recruiter to have several people eligible to join the Navy, but who can't because of their category."

Recruiters who are not successful in meeting their quotas risk being transferred out of recruiting—an action that can place a dark cloud over someone's military future.

The Training of Recruiters

When the threat of the draft was removed, the recruiter's job became more difficult. Each branch overhauled its training programs. The training manuals now used in recruiters' school are filled with sales terms such as "prospecting for leads," "buying motives," "overcoming objections," and "closing the sale." A current Army publication for recruiters states, "We are salesmen in every sense of the word. There are techniques that you must use to ensure that you don't find yourself an unsuccessful salesman."

As a sales "prospect," you should be aware that recruiters are often highly skilled at presenting their "product" (military service) in the most appealing terms. Like any salesperson, a recruiter will work hard to convince you of the benefits of enlisting, while downplaying any concerns that you may raise.

OUTREACH TO YOUTH

In addition to advertising, the armed forces use a number of other techniques to reach likely recruiting prospects. Some of the more significant programs are described below.

Direct Mail Marketing

The Pentagon currently sends *19 million* pieces of bulk mail to the homes of sixteen- to twenty-one-year-olds each year. They try a wide variety of mailing lists, everything from "teen" magazines to motor vehicle ownership records. Lt. Col. John Cullen, of the Army's Recruiting Command, told me an interesting story about one such test. The Army mailed recruiting material to a list of buyers of an exercise device called "The Bullworker." Although the response was good, the list had to be dropped. It turned out that this product was also used by many disabled people, who complained that the military was mocking their condition by sending them recruiting material.

These mailings commonly offer a free gift as an incentive to return the postage-paid response card. The Army has found that when it offers a pair of tube socks or a wall poster, it receives five times as many responses. When your free gift is mailed, so is your name and address to recruiters in your hometown. These half-million "leads" furnished to the recruiters each year are a rich source of enlistment prospects.

Futures *Magazine*

Published for the military by Scholastic Magazines, this glossy, full-color magazine is mailed free of charge to three million high school seniors each fall. It features short articles on vocational and career issues along with numerous recruiting ads. The reader is invited to fill out a short questionnaire and to return it to the magazine. Respondents' names and addresses are sent to local recruiters.

Armed Services Vocational Aptitude Battery (ASVAB) Test

About 1.25 million students at 14,000 high schools and community colleges take this general aptitude test each year. Most schools give the test during school hours, although participation is voluntary. In some districts, however, students are required to take the ASVAB. Each school district can decide whether test results will be given to local recruiters without students' consent.

Although attitudes toward recruiters' access to the schools varies from town to town and state to state, the current policy in New York State is probably typical. The Education Department, "encourages close cooperation between the schools and military recruiters." The use of the ASVAB is "encouraged to assist counselors and recruiters accomplish the proper placement of students who are interested in joining the [military]."

School Directories and Class Lists

After the postage-paid "response" cards and the ASVAB results, school directories and class lists are the recruiters' best sources of leads.

Referrals by Educators and Counselors

Recruiters today try to establish good relationships with high school personnel. In years past, they would sometimes turn off teachers by encouraging students to quit school to enlist. Today, since none of the branches will enlist more than a small percentage of nongraduates, recruiters encourage students to get their diplomas first.

One way that recruiters make friends is by providing some teachers with expense-paid trips to various military bases. The Army sends over 1,100 educators on such base visits each year. The other branches also operate similar programs.

Junior Reserve Officer Training Corps (JROTC)

About 130,000 high school students currently serve in 1,500 JROTC units throughout the United States. These units sometimes sponsor school visits by special parachute or helicopter teams that demonstrate military tactics and weaponry.

Referrals by Recent Recruits

Almost everyone who enlists today signs a "Delayed Entry Program (DEP)" contract in which they promise to report for active duty up to a year later. During the DEP period, enlistees are encouraged by recruiters to provide names of friends and relatives who might consider enlistment. If any of these people join, the referring person receives an accelerated promotion to the rank of private (E/2) after basic training. (Each enlisted person is assigned a pay rating ranging from E/1 to E/9). Both the Navy and the Marines operate a program whereby recent training graduates return to their hometowns for a limited period to assist recruiters in signing up others. About 400 sailors participate in the Navy's program at any given time. They contact their friends, speak at local schools and clubs, and generally "sell" the Navy.

Referrals Between Recruiters

If a Navy recruiter cannot "qualify" a candidate, he may pass the name of that person along to a recruiter from another military branch that may have different entrance standards. These kinds of referrals are common among recruiters from all the branches.

In summary, it's a safe bet that if you express the slightest interest in military service, you will be pursued eagerly by one or more recruiters. You can decide at any time that you don't want to continue discussing things with a recruiter. If you decide that you're no longer interested, just tell the recruiter. The Army provides a toll-free number (1-800-872-7321) that you can call to complain about any Army recruiter. For the Navy, call 1-800-327-NAVY.

FIVE TIPS FOR NEGOTIATING WITH RECRUITERS

Take Along a Parent or Adult Friend

Take along one of your parents or an adult friend when you first visit the recruiter's office. Recruiters should be happy to explain service opportunities to both of you. If a dispute later develops over exactly what was said or promised, it won't be just your word against his. Also, you may be a little intimidated by someone who wears a uniform and talks with great confidence. Your adult companion may be able to ask some questions that you don't think of.

Don't Sign Anything on Your First Visit

Don't sign anything at the recruiting station until you or your companion are sure exactly what it means. It's best to take any papers home where you can read them over more carefully. Recruiters have been known to say that papers cannot be taken out of the office. However, once you have enlisted, you are entitled to a copy of your enlistment contract, so why shouldn't you be allowed to look it over at home *before* you sign? You will also be asked to sign a permission form allowing your recruiter to check on your school, job, or possible police records.

Shop Around

You wouldn't buy the first car that you were shown on a dealer's lot, would you? Then why would you commit yourself after talking with only one recruiter? Make an effort to find out what each of the service branches can offer you. Sometimes a recruiter from one branch will tell you that you are not qualified for another branch. Why not find out for yourself? Also, a recruiter might offer you a better deal in terms of training or assignment if he knows you're considering offers from other service branches.

Don't Allow Yourself to Be Pressured

Don't let yourself be rushed or pressured by the recruiter. Sometimes a prospect is told that unless he enlists right away, he will
miss a deadline for a particular training program or assignment.
Don't let such concerns stampede you into making a hasty
commitment.

A tragic example of what can happen when someone makes a
hasty commitment is illustrated by the case of John Heim of
Nanuet, NY. A high school dropout, John had called a local
Navy recruiter on a whim one afternoon in January 1988. Within
an hour, the recruiter arrived at John's home. Even though
John's mother asked the recruiter to stay and discuss the Navy's
programs with the family, he ushered John to the door, explaining that this could be done only at the recruiting station. Later
that night, the recruiter brought John home, after arranging to
pick him up at 6:00 AM the next morning. John was kept busy
from dawn to dusk the next two days at the Military Entrance
Processing Station (MEPS), undergoing physical and mental exams, aptitude testing, and completing all the administrative details of enlistment. Less than three days after he'd first tele-
phoned the recruiter, John was on his way to basic training with
a four-year service obligation. John later told his parents that he
had signed so quickly because he had been told there was a
deadline for the kind of training program he wanted.

According to his parents, Kathy and Wayland, John was miserable from the moment he arrived at basic training. Each night he
called home, with every call becoming more desperate than the
last. Because he never had the chance to pause and think about
how his personal dislike of physical conditioning and of being
under strict control twenty-four hours a day was incompatible
with military life, John's hasty decision led to tragedy.

When John's parents expressed their worries about their son to
his base commander, he told them to stop "babying" their son.
When John was denied leave to visit his critically ill grandparents,
it may have pushed him over the edge. Despondent, he hung himself in his barracks on May 16, 1988.

Get All Promises in Writing on Your Contract

Make sure that any promises as to training, assignment, bonuses, etc., appear in writing on your enlistment contract before you sign it. Verbal promises are worthless. At the bottom of the front page of the enlistment contract, the following appears: "The agreements in this section and attached annex(es) are all the promises made to me ... ANYTHING ELSE ANYONE HAS PROMISED ME IS NOT VALID AND WILL NOT BE HONORED." Don't rely on verbal promises like, "you can request that once you are at basic training."

A VISIT TO THE RECRUITERS

Now that you know how to protect yourself, it's time to pay a visit to the recruiters. Accompanied by your trusty adult friend or parent, you venture forth. Incidentally, no one under the age of seventeen can enlist. The written consent of *both* parents (if they are reasonably available) or a guardian is required for anyone between seventeen and eighteen.

After an exchange of pleasantries, the recruiter will ask you to sit next to him at a computer console. Recruiters today use a video system that the military calls the Joint Optical Information Network (JOIN). This system provides the recruiter with up-to-the-minute job-opening and training possibilities. Remember, however, that what is available may have changed by the time you visit the Military Entrance Processing Station (MEPS) where the actual selection of assignment takes place.

The recruiter most likely will ask you to watch a video featuring a short program about the service branch he represents. He will then ask you to take a short test, with questions similar in difficulty to those on the ASVAB test. The questions will be displayed on the monitor, and you will use the computer keyboard to type in your answers. The questions will increase in difficulty until you give a wrong answer. The computer will then set all subsequent questions at just below that level of difficulty. When the test is finished, the recruiter will give you the results immediately, and will interpret what they mean in terms of your aptitude and skills.

If the recruiter thinks you can qualify for enlistment, he will then check to see if you have taken the ASVAB test. Everyone who enlists in the military must take this three-hour aptitude test. If you haven't, he will schedule you to do so at a Military Entrance Test Site (METS) as close to your home as possible. Most urban areas will have several METS locations, often in federal office buildings. Metropolitan New York has ten sites, for example.

Next, he will ask you questions about your career and educational goals, work experience, family situation, sports interests, and hobbies. If you're interested in a specific military program, the Navy's Nuclear Power School for example, the recruiter will arrange for you to take a specialized test designed to measure your aptitude in that area.

Assuming that you continue to show interest, the recruiter will enter data into his computer about the benefits the military can offer you. If he is an Army recruiter, he will present you with a customized form entitled, "Potential Benefits Summary Sheet," which will have your name at the top. This will list the total dollars in college assistance that you will receive, based on the length of enlistment. If you qualify for other payments, such as enlistment bonuses, the Army's College Fund, repayment of college loans, etc., these will be calculated as well. The form will list a "job category" that you have selected, because this often determines payment eligibility. Don't forget that this is *only* a "dream sheet." No promise of training or assignment is binding on the military unless it has been typed into your enlistment contract and signed by the appropriate military official.

This form will also summarize the total amount that you will receive as salary and the estimated value of housing and food that you'll receive during your enlistment period. The recruiter also will point out numerous other benefits, such as free medical care, legal assistance, shopping privileges at PX's and commissaries, thirty days annual vacation, and cheap insurance. Although this document looks official, it is purely advisory and *does not* commit the military to anything.

A Word of Advice

The enlistment application contains a series of questions about criminal convictions and arrests, juvenile court problems, and minor offenses, including traffic violations or turnstile jumping (fare evasion). It also asks if you have ever been fired, arrested, or treated for alcoholism. Finally, the form asks if you are a homosexual, a conscientious objector (pacifist), or if you have served previously in any branch of the military.

It is important that you answer each question fully and honestly. Recruiters have been known to suggest that you leave something out if they know that it might make you ineligible for enlistment. If the concealed fact is later disclosed, the blame will fall on you—the recruiter won't be around.

Assuming that your aptitude scores and educational level qualify you for enlistment, the recruiter will work hard to complete the enlistment application and to prepare you for your visit to the MEPS.

Important Note:

Many young people and their parents don't understand exactly what recruiters can and cannot do. A recruiter's job is to identify young people who are interested in military service, to advise them about career opportunities in the military, and to sign qualified prospects to enlistment contracts. However, a military recruiter *cannot* enlist anyone into the military. If you change your mind about going on active duty *before* you take the second oath of service at the MEPS on reporting day, you are under *no obligation*—no matter how much time the recruiter spent working with you. You do *not* have to accompany the recruiter to the MEPS for either the preliminary screening or on the date you promised to go on active duty. You have no obligation to talk with anyone else in the military about your decision! (See Chapter 7 for more details.)

Anything a recruiter has promised you about training and assignment is subject to approval by personnel at the MEPS. It is not uncommon for a young person to go to the MEPS expecting to be assigned to train in a specific field, only to find out that there are no openings or that he doesn't qualify for one reason or another.

The Importance of the ASVAB Test

The military uses your composite scores from the ASVAB test as a principal means of determining your eligibility for various training programs and assignments. The test is designed to evaluate a prospect's abilities compared to all others who take the test. It consists of ten parts: Mathematics Knowledge; Arithmetic Reasoning; Reading Comprehension; Word Knowledge; Mechanical Comprehension; Electronics Information; General Science; Auto and Shop Information; Paragraph Comprehension; and Numerical Operations. Recruits must score well above average on the first four parts if they hope to qualify for highly technical skills training.

Test results are divided into seven composite aptitude scores, three "academic" and four "occupational." The latter are divided into four categories: Mechanical and Crafts; Business and Clerical; Electronics and Electrical; and Health, Social, and Technology. The military claims that the "occupational" scores help to predict one's potential for training in a number of career areas, while the "academic" scores measure one's aptitude for higher education. One overall score, called the AFQT Score, is also provided.

The military states that the ASVAB test helps school counselors advise their students about career choices, even if they are not considering military service. However, high school counselors today are often responsible for so many students that they're unable to provide much individual counseling. My impression is that few schools make independent use of the ASVAB test results. It is primarily a tool for recruiters to identify likely prospects.

The military works hard to have the ASVAB test given by as many high schools and community colleges as possible. One of the Army's recruiting manuals explains why: "Few sales organizations survive without a constant source of leads. Your ASVAB program is the seed from which your best leads will come. The amazing thing about the [ASVAB] is that you receive mentally prequalified leads . . . what would hundreds of prequalified leads be worth to you? Many recruiters have already discovered [that] mandatory ASVAB testing can convert a very difficult task into a pleasurable project."

If you are interested in joining the military, you should try to score as high as you can on the test. For many years, Arco has published a useful study guide called *Practice for the Armed Forces Test–ASVAB* by Solomon Wiener ($9.95), which is available in most bookstores.

The military uses four of the subtests to calculate your overall AFQT score: Word Knowledge; Paragraph Comprehension; Arithmetic Reasoning; and Numerical Operations.

AFQT scores are ranked as follows:

Category I	93–99	
Category II	65–92	
Category IIIA	50–64	(50 is considered a minimum score for many jobs requiring skills training.)
Category IIIB	31–49	
Category IV	10–30	(Only a limited number of these can be enlisted.)
Category V	1–9	(Not eligible for enlistment.)

At present, about 38 percent of the men and 40 percent of the women who take the test score in the top two mental categories. ASVAB test scores are valid for two years from the time you take the test. If you think you can improve your score the second time around, you can take it again after a six months' wait. Sometimes recruiters will encourage a prospect to retake the test when they feel that his score is abnormally low.

YOUR VISITS TO THE MILITARY ENTRANCE PROCESSING STATION (MEPS)

Once your recruiter has completed all of the paperwork and has received reports on your school work, employment history, and possible police record, he will arrange for you to visit the MEPS. All the armed services use this same network of MEPS facilities to process recruits. Enlisted men and officers, Reservists and National Guard members are all seen at these centers. There are currently sixty-eight MEPS centers throughout the country, with almost every state having at least one. They are primarily located in large cities.

You will make two visits to the MEPS center. On the first visit, you will be given a physical examination, receive your military assignment, and be sworn into the Reserves. When you return again, you will be placed on active duty and leave for basic training.

YOUR FIRST VISIT TO THE MEPS

Normally, your recruiter will make travel arrangements for your visits to the MEPS. If you don't live too far from a processing station, he will usually escort you on the morning of your appointment. If it is a long journey, say 100 miles or more, the recruiter may give you a bus or train ticket and arrange for you to stay overnight at a hotel near the MEPS. As a rule, recruiters like to "shepherd" their enlistees. When a *Navy Times* reporter recently asked a recruiter why he rose before dawn to drive recruits to the MEPS, his reply was blunt: "You lose too many enlistees on the bus." Air Force and Coast Guard officials say that they discourage their recruiters from this practice.

Your Physical Examination

You will arrive at the MEPS as dawn is breaking. First, you'll be shown a short video that will explain what will happen that day. Next, you'll be given a thorough physical examination that will take about two and a half hours. The recruiter will have already had you fill out a detailed medical history. The MEPS medical staff will check your condition against these forms, looking for possible problems. If you have suffered a health problem in the past, such as a sports injury, it is a good idea to bring a letter from your doctor stating that you are no longer affected by the condition.

If a health problem such as a vision or hearing defect is detected, the MEPS doctors will usually determine on the spot whether or not it affects your eligibility. In some cases, they may ask you to see a specialist before they will allow you to enlist. If you are found medically ineligible, your processing will be terminated.

Because today's military stresses fitness among all its members, your weight and height must fall within prescribed limits. If you are unusually muscular, the MEPS staff will measure your percentage of body fat because you may qualify for an extra weight allowance. If your weight falls just over or under the limits, you may be allowed to come back later for another weighing, assuming you are willing to try to lose (or gain) the required pounds.

A Word of Caution

Since June 1988, the MEPS have been required to test each applicant for exposure to the AIDS virus by analyzing your blood for
the presence of the HIV-III antibody, and for alcohol abuse by
administering a breathalyzer test. The MEPS uses a standard that
will rate you intoxicated at half the alcohol level used in most
states to arrest drunk drivers. Go easy with those preenlistment
parties!

If the blood test finds you to be "positive" for the HIV-III antibody, you will receive a registered letter asking you to return to
the MEPS to "discuss your processing." A MEPS doctor and the
commander will personally inform you that you are "positive"
and are therefore ineligible for enlistment. This does *not* mean
that you will automatically develop AIDS or the AIDS-related
Complex (ARC), although there is a serious risk of this. You may
want to contact a counseling group that works with AIDS
"positives" in your community to obtain additional medical
information.

Your Meeting With a Guidance Counselor

After you complete your physical examination, you will be sent
for an interview with a guidance counselor who works for the
service branch you are joining. This session is what a novelist
might call your "moment of truth." During this brief encounter,
which usually lasts no more than twenty minutes, your military
fate will be decided, at least in terms of skills training and
assignment.

This counselor will look over your enlistment packet and then
talk with you briefly about your preferences for training and assignment. If your recruiter promised you that you would receive
a certain kind of training, tell the job counselor this. He will then
enter this information into a computer, along with your test
scores. Overall, this system works somewhat like an airline reser-
vation system. A training slot or assignment that is "open" when
the computer is turned on in the morning may disappear fifteen
minutes later when counselors at other MEPS centers "reserve"
it for their enlistees.

My impressions, based on observing a MEPS counselor, is that
the military likes to use these computers to convey a sense of
inevitability about the assignment process. In other words, the

enlistee is encouraged to think that whatever appears on the computer screen is final and that no negotiation is possible. For example, PFC Joe Wojak, a crane operator at Fort Bragg, NC, was told by his counselor that "the computer" offered only two choices; field artillery or heavy equipment operation, even though his recruiter had mentioned other options.

If you make it clear to the counselor that you will enlist only if you are offered a promise of training that interests you, I think he may work harder to satisfy you. In some cases, you simply may lack the qualifications required by a certain career field, but it won't hurt to try. The counselor may give you the impression that the computer has the final word, but it ain't necessarily so.

Previous run-ins with the law over alcohol or drug use may bar you from certain assignments, such as those in the nuclear field. You can seek a waiver if you have an otherwise clean record. Decisions about waivers are made on a case-by-case basis by officers who are stationed at the MEPS.

Sometimes a job counselor will apply pressure by warning you that if you don't sign now, you will miss out on your second or third job choices as well. Don't "settle" for something else, if there is only one job that will satisfy you. If you are offered nothing that appeals to you, you can always go home without enlisting. You do *not* have to enlist, no matter how much this disappoints your recruiter. Of course, if you leave without enlisting, your recruiter may decide to have nothing more to do with you.

Although there are more similarities than differences in the way job counselors of the different branches operate, there are some distinctions that you should know about.

ARMY COUNSELORS

All of the Army's "guidance counselors" are former recruiters, so they tend to skilled in the art of persuasion. The Army breaks down its 300 entry-level jobs into thirty-three "career management fields (CMF)." At any given time, many of these will not be open for new enlistees. Bear in mind that even though the military relies on technology more than ever, thousands of combat jobs must still be filled. Out of 970,000 people currently serving in the Army and the Marines, at least one quarter serve in the combat arms. This means that one out of four marches in the infantry, rides in a tank, parachutes out of airplanes, or fires artillery howitzers. Although the television ads can make them look almost glamorous, these jobs are just as difficult, dirty, and potentially as dangerous as ever.

Many other military jobs have little application to the civilian job market. For example, the military has 60,000 "ordnance mechanics" today. The official *Military Career Guide* lists as "helpful personal attributes" for this job; "an interest in working with explosives and the ability to remain calm [!]" For an in-depth discussion of military jobs and civilian employment, see Chapter 3.

In addition to promises concerning job training and assignment, an Army counselor can offer one or more of the following programs for those who qualify:

GI Bill (All branches offer this)

If a recruit authorizes a nonrefundable payroll deduction of $100 a month for a year, he'll qualify for $9,600 in college aid on a three- or four-year enlistment. These payments are not made in a lump sum however, but are spread out over thirty-six months. To receive money, the former servicemember must be registered for a minimum number of credits and must receive passing grades. Because college tuition costs have escalated rapidly in recent years, GI Bill payments cover only a portion of expenses. Probably for this reason, only a small percentage of service veterans ever use their GI Bill benefits.

Army College Fund

If a GI with a high school diploma serves in a "critical skill" area and has an AFQT score of at least 50, he will receive $12,000 in college aid for a three-year enlistment and $14,400 for a four year enlistment. This money is paid in *addition* to the GI Bill. Army jobs for which the College Fund was recently paid are: tank turret repairer, combat signaler, power generator repairer, and petroleum supply specialist. These are only examples. The list of "critical skills" changes constantly based on the Army's needs. Like the GI Bill, payments under this program are made on a monthly basis and require passing grades in a mandatory number of courses.

Student Loan Repayment Program

The Army will repay 33 percent or $1,500, whichever is greater, of outstanding federal student loan debt for each year that a recruit serves in a "critical-skills" job. GI's who receive this benefit are ineligible for the GI Bill program.

Cash Bonuses for Enlistment (All branches offer this)

Bonuses ranging from $1,500 to $8,000 are paid to selected recruits who enlist for two types of jobs: those that are least desirable (combat arms), and those that require technical skills that are in short supply. Often the bonus is paid in installments over the entire contract, not as a lump sum. You must sign a three- or four-year contract and have an AFQT of 50 or higher to qualify.

Two-Year Enlistment

The Army is the only branch (except for the Coast Guard) that still offers this short contract. Only 3,500 out of about 120,000 recruits who enter the Army each year choose the two-year obligation. The average Army Enlistment contract is for three years, with five additional years spent in the Individual Ready Reserves (an inactive force).

NAVY COUNSELORS

The Navy organizes its entry-level jobs into seventy different "ratings." The Navy's counselors at the MEP work in a manner similar to the Army's counselors. You should remember that assignment to a specific training program (called "A" Schools in the Navy) means only that you will be enrolled. It's entirely up to you to meet all the course requirements. In recent years, the drop-out rate from some of the Navy's "A" Schools has exceeded 40 percent. In an effort to reduce attrition, the schools have implemented various reforms, including the simplification of some course material.

The Navy counselors will not provide you with a guarantee of your first duty station. However, according to a Navy spokesperson at the MEPS in New York City, at least 80 percent of all first-term sailors are assigned to sea duty.

The average length of Navy enlistment is four years, with four additional years in the inactive Reserves.

MARINE COUNSELORS

A popular saying in the Corps is, "every Marine a rifleman." This means that each Marine, no matter what his rank or job, has qualified as a combat infantryman. The Marines historically have functioned as a mobile amphibious ground combat force, and all Marines are expected to enthusiastically share the warrior values of the small but fiercely proud Corps.

This philosophy extends to the manner in which Marine Corps recruits are enlisted. According to Major DeCamp, recruiting chief for the Marines on Long Island, NY, "the liaison [counselor] is not at the MEPS to sell a job or put a guy into a certain program. We sell the Marines as a force that builds character, values, maturity, a way of meeting challenges, and working to meet your potential. My recruiters don't tell people that we're preparing them for an esoteric job when they get out."

According to Marine Corps headquarters, "Our promises (to enlistees), if any, are general in nature. No specific guarantees for occupational assignment or duty station are made." About 16 percent of enlistees enter under the Quality Enlistment Program or the Quality Enlistment Bonus, under which they are guaranteed either specific training, a specific duty station, or paid a bonus for enlisting. The rest are enlisted without specific promises of training or assignment, although their preferences later will be matched with the needs of the Marines.

In one recent case handled by my associate, Louis Font of Boston, a young Marine, John Requelme, was promised training in top-secret Signals Intelligence work and a $4,000 bonus. Once on active duty, the Marine Corps discovered that Requelme's father resided in a foreign country (Paraguay). They ruled that his non-citizen parent made John ineligible for the necessary security clearance, even though he had listed his father's citizenship on his enlistment application. Only after a lengthy (and expensive) legal battle was Requelme discharged.

The average Marine enlistment is for four to six years. About 79 percent of enlistees join for four years; 9 percent for five years; and 12 percent for six years. Quality Enlistment may require a five- to six-year commitment.

AIR FORCE COUNSELORS

Tech. Sgt. John LaBelle, who supervises the Air Force MEPS counselors in New York, explains that recruiters are encouraged to sell the Air Force as a way of life, rather than a specific promise of job training. Recruits are enlisted in a general area, such as mechanics or administration, rather than being promised a specific job. They are assigned to specific technical schools once basic training is completed. The Air Force will take recruits' preferences into account in making these assignments. "We've found that young people often don't know exactly what they're interested in until they've been on active duty for a while," LaBelle explains.

Colonel William Sheppard, Vice Commander of Air Force Recruiting Headquarters at Randolph AFB, TX, told me that although a specific promise of job training is sometimes made depending on the applicant's qualifications, commitments of duty station are made only infrequently as an incentive to fill unpopular jobs.

The average length of Air Force enlistment is four years, with four additional years in the inactive Reserves. About 10 percent enlist for six years, with two more years in the inactive Reserves. Six-year enlistees are given rapid promotion to E-3 after basic training.

COAST GUARD COUNSELORS

This service operates somewhat differently from the other branches. It relies on its recruiters to discuss job training possibilities with prospective recruits. No training assignments are made at the MEPS. Instead, the Coast Guard has a policy of sending every recruit to a regular unit for a few months after they complete basic training.

"We want individuals to go out with a unit for a while so that they can see what the various jobs are like before choosing a school," explains Chief Petty Officer Wind, a recruiting spokesperson in New York. The Coast Guard adopted this system after finding that many recruits were dissatisfied with training choices they had made sight unseen.

The small size of this branch requires it to offer more generalized training to its recruits. "Our schools give you a wider background in many types of equipment and job skills than the other services," states Chief Wind. "Our yeomen assigned to clerical work will do everything from service records to payroll to travel requests, instead of just one task."

The average length of Coast Guard enlistment is four years, plus four years in the inactive Reserves. Two-year enlistments are also offered in some instances. However, those who enlist on the short contract receive no promise of training or assignment.

Important Information About the Delayed Entry Enlistment Contract:

On your first visit to the MEPS, you may sign an enlistment contract that places you in the Delayed Entry Program (DEP). Under this contract, you promise to report for enlistment into active duty on a specific date, up to one year in the future. The contract states, "I understand that I will be ordered to active duty as a Reservist unless I report to the place shown by [reporting date]."

I interpret the relevant regulations to mean that the armed forces do not have the legal authority to "order" these enlistees to active duty. Technically, people in the DEP are assigned to the Individual Ready Reserve (IRR). As such, they are not assigned to any military unit, nor do they attend any drills or wear a uniform. Only when you take the oath of service at the MEPS during your *second* visit do you legally place yourself on active duty and subject yourself to military authority.

Spokespeople for each service branch explain that it is against official policy to force anyone in the Delayed Entry Program onto active duty against their will. Down in the trenches, where the recruiters operate, however, it's often a different story. See Chapter 9 for a detailed discussion of DEP contracts.

YOUR SECOND VISIT TO THE MEPS

On your second visit to the MEPS, you will undergo a last-minute check of your health status and documents. You then will be sworn into active duty and usually will depart for your basic training assignment on the same day. If you have serious questions about your earlier decision to enlist, you should *not* return to the MEPS. Consult Chapter 9, instead.

RECRUITMENT OF OFFICERS

The military makes a very important distinction between commissioned officers and enlisted personnel. Officers enjoy a special social status, as well as benefits and privileges that are not available to enlisted members. Officers function as both the middle-level managers and top leadership for the entire military system. As such, they can exercise great power and authority over those serving below them. On the other hand, they are expected to meet higher standards of personal conduct than enlisted persons. For instance, just one "positive" urinalysis for drug use will end an officer's career, whereas an enlisted person will sometimes get a second chance.

With a few exceptions, only persons with a four-year college degree and who are U.S. citizens are eligible to become commissioned officers. Officer candidates must meet the same standards of physical qualifications as enlisted personnel.

Today, there are basically four ways to become an officer. They are listed below.

Service Academies

The most prestigious way to receive an officer's commission is by graduating from one of the five service academies; West Point (Army), Annapolis (Navy), the Air Force, the Coast Guard, or the Merchant Marine. These four-year colleges provide their cadets with an all-expenses-paid education, plus second lieutenant's bars (or the equivalent) when they graduate. The academies offer a regular college curriculum, although it is heavily weighted towards science, math, and technical subjects. Although much of the course material is similar to a regular college, a definite "military" atmosphere pervades each of the five institutions. Summers are spent undergoing rigorous military training at various military installations.

Academy graduates enjoy a special status within their respective service branches. Most military people believe that an informal network of academy grads (sometimes called "ringknockers") exists to help members with promotion and assignments.

About 11 percent of all Army officers in 1984 were academy grads, yet 34 percent of all generals went to West Point!

The biggest obstacle for those who are interested in attending the academies is their restricted enrollment. In 1984, for example, West Point admitted just 1,515 out of almost 17,000 applications. For the Navy, 1,329 were accepted out of 12,614 who applied.

Once admitted, many cadets find the high-pressure, competitive atmosphere a difficult adjustment. All of the academies stress athletic prowess. For instance, 80 percent of a recent graduating class from Annapolis had been varsity letter–winners in high school.

At present, about one in four cadets at West Point fails to graduate. If you quit before your junior year, no military obligation is incurred. Theoretically, a cadet who resigns during or after his junior year can be ordered to active duty as an enlisted person. I was told however, that this is not done at present.

If you wish to apply to a service academy, you should contact the school that you're interested in early in your junior year of high school. You will need to get an elected official, usually a member of Congress, to endorse your application. Each academy has liaison officers throughout the United States who can help you work through the complicated application process. The academies will provide you with their names and addresses when you write for application information.

The Army operates a special school at Fort Monmouth, NJ, that helps about 150 enlisted people to prepare for admission to West Point each year. The school offers an intensified ten-month course of study in a variety of academic subjects, as well as physical conditioning. The program is open to unmarried high school graduates between the ages of seventeen and twenty-one who are currently on active duty. All who complete the course are nominated for West Point; most will receive appointments as cadets.

Reserve Officer Training Corps (ROTC)

This is the military's single largest source of officers today. About 1,350 colleges and universities throughout the United States offer ROTC programs, which account for almost 40 percent of the military's new officers. Schools offer Army, Navy, or Air Force programs; some offer all three.

Each service operates a separate recruiting command for its ROTC program. The Army calls these recruiters "gold-mining teams," referring to the gold bars that second lieutenants wear. These teams spend most of their time on college campuses trying to recruit freshmen and sophomores into the program. Although they employ some of the same techniques described earlier, they try to adopt a style that blends in with the college environment. Recently commissioned second lieutenants are often sent back to their alma maters to spend a few months helping sign new cadets.

One problem for the military has been the low status of ROTC duty among most career military people. Recently, there have been attempts to upgrade the "image" of ROTC duty to allay fears that these assignments may harm one's chances for promotion.

College students enlist for two-, three-, or four-year ROTC programs, depending on the service branch they choose. Legally, there are two separate parts to the ROTC program. During the first two years, ROTC cadets attend training and drills as volunteers, although they receive some college credit for the classroom work. During this period, cadets can quit the programs at will with no military obligation.

The second phase, which usually begins with the junior year, requires that cadets sign an enlistment contract that places them on Reserve status. All cadets now receive a monthly paycheck and other allowances. In addition, many receive partial or full academic scholarships for college expenses.

If a cadet fails to perform satisfactorily or quits during this phase, the military claims to have the authority to place him on active duty to serve out his obligation as an enlisted person. If you find yourself in this situation, you should contact one of the organizations listed in the Appendix and obtain the names of experienced lawyers in your area.

Sometimes college graduates are talked into joining the military as enlisted personnel. Recruiters sometimes argue that it is a good experience to "start at the bottom" and that enlisted personnel can attend Officers Candidate School (OCS). Actually, the competition for admission to OCS is quite intense. Most college graduates who've gone this route would probably enter as officers if they could do it over again!

Officers Candidate Schools

Each service branch operates special schools that train enlisted personnel, and warrant officers with college degrees and non-ROTC college graduates to become commissioned officers. As I mentioned, competition for entrance is usually fierce, and only those with outstanding service records are normally admitted.

The Marines offer commissions to a select number of enlisted people who have only two years of college provided they are between the ages of twenty-one and twenty-six.

Direct Appointment

Doctors, lawyers, dentists, engineers, priests, and ministers who are certified in their respective fields may be eligible for direct commissioning as officers. They immediately begin practicing their professions once on active duty with only a minimum amount of military training. About 13 percent of new officers receive their commissions in this way.

Chapter 2

Basic Training

Basic training is not what it used to be; but then, what is? The horror stories you may have heard from your father or uncles about sadistic drill instructors (DI's) don't have much validity today. Basic training still is demanding mentally and physically, but the beatings and punishment marches that were fairly common twenty or thirty years ago are now outlawed.

Incidents in which recruits are abused still do occur from time to time. Two Air Force instructors were removed from their jobs in August 1988 at Lackland AFB, TX, for knocking a hole in a wall with a recruit's head and jamming a pen up the nose of another. In March 1989, the Navy admitted to a Congressional agency probing the highly publicized death of recruit Lee Mirecki during swim training that sixteen other sailors also had been killed during training in the previous three years.

Today, all of the services have strict rules against the physical abuse of recruits. The drill instructor schools I visited at Fort Dix, NJ, and Parris Island, SC, both stress the hands-off rule in their courses. Nevertheless, the near-total control that drill instructors have over recruits creates an environment in which frustration and anger may occasionally escalate into abuse.

One drill instructor at Fort Dix told me that despite the rules against corporal punishment, DI's still have methods of making life miserable for errant recruits. He mentioned assigning extra duty, taking away free time or telephone privileges, and issuing counseling statements as examples. In addition, all the services allow their DI's (with some restrictions) to give "physical incentives" to recruits, meaning extra push-ups, sit-ups, and other calisthenics as punishment. The Marines call the sandpit where their recruits do "incentive" training the "rose garden."

Although the physical screening enlistees undergo should detect most health problems in advance, the stress of vigorous exercise can be hazardous. The investigation of the seventeen Navy training deaths found that five of them occurred during strenuous exercise, such as long-distance running.

In just one month, September 1988, the Army lost two soldiers, Private Jeffrey Tuck of Holliston, MA, and Sgt. John Hull of Keyser, WV, both of whom collapsed and died during training runs at two different bases. Concerned about the growing number of injuries, particularly stress fractures, the Army announced in May 1989 that henceforth, recruits will take a break from running during the third week of basic.

About five years ago, the Army revamped its basic training by getting rid of the "high stress" approach, in which DI's constantly criticized recruits for their shortcomings. This was replaced with a program of "positive" leadership, whereby DI's try to encourage and motivate recruits. The evaluation period for recruits was also lengthened, giving them a better chance to prove themselves. There has also been an effort to pick DI's who have more rank and experience than those in the past.

However, despite these changes, DI's still follow the practice of singling out a few recruits who are overweight or clumsy for harassment as a warning to the others.

DI's also rely on peer pressure to encourage obedience. Instructors will sometimes punish a whole training unit for the failure of one or two trainees to pass inspection. In the movie *Full Metal Jacket*, the DI vents his anger about one recruit's performance on his fellow trainees. The hapless GI is then viciously beaten by the rest of his comrades during a "blanket party." Today, such a party would be forbidden, unless, of course, the DI's didn't know about it. Training units also are encouraged to compete with each other for awards and privileges, adding to the pressure.

One reason instructors encourage peer pressure is that a number of studies have documented that GI's fight best when they are fighting for the safety of their unit and for the respect of their fellow soldiers.

Although the basic training conducted by each of the services varies according to that branch's traditions and mission, there are common objectives that can be summarized as follows:

- To teach recruits to respect the chain of command. One reason for this indoctrination is to condition trainees to automatically obey orders from superiors.

- To develop a strong identification with the unit, while downplaying individual concerns.

- To develop physical fitness so that it inspires personal confidence.

The Marine Corps' description of its basic training goals is "to indoctrinate recruits in the fundamentals of service life, to develop discipline, proficiency in general military subjects, and love of Corps and country." The Air Force uses basic to "give recruits an opportunity to grow into young adults . . . . They learn teamwork, discipline, and the need for self-control and self-discipline."

The Marines have the reputation of having the most difficult basic. It lasts the longest (thirteen weeks for men), and one out of six recruits (men and women) fails to finish it—the highest failure rate of any branch, although the Coast Guard, with a 14 percent rate, ranks just behind.

The commander of Marine drill instructor school told me that many young people join the Marines because they want a "challenge." According to this officer, "Most recruits say that they thought basic would be worse than it was."

Some military experts question whether the American military devotes enough time to combat training. The British and Israeli armies, for example, put their soldiers through twenty-two weeks of combat training.

The basic offered by the Army and Navy is considered to be somewhat less demanding, although between 8–10 percent of those who enter fail. The Air Force, which has the shortest basic, also has the lowest failure rate. For instance, its trainees spend only one day on the rifle range and are not required to camp out in tents even a single night. But then, the Air Force trains its people to work around high-tech equipment or to fly airplanes, not to march with rifle and pack and fight from foxholes.

My impression is that almost anyone who is reasonably fit can complete basic successfully, provided he maintains the proper mental attitude. You should make up your mind that you will promptly obey all orders with an air of feigned (if not real) enthusiasm. Above all, try to blend into the crowd and avoid drawing attention to yourself.

A brochure the Navy gives to new recruits sums up the philosophy: "Allow yourself to be guided completely in all matters by your company commanders [DI's]. Decide that you'll do exactly what they tell you to do, when they tell you to do it. Obedience to authority is the first necessary attitude to adopt."

I relate the following story to illustrate what sometimes can (and does) happen to a young man or woman during training, even though there may be nothing in their past to suggest that they couldn't handle the stress.

I was contacted by Mrs. Jennifer LeBarron of Pittsfield, MA. Her son, Trevor, had entered Army basic at Fort Benning, GA, in September 1987, hoping to become a helicopter pilot. In high school, he had been a popular member of the varsity football team. Something went very wrong during Trevor's first few days of basic. Although the full story is still not known, he was found late one night wandering in front of his barracks, wearing only a blanket, after he had apparently pulled a fire alarm that roused his entire training company. Two other recruits later told Trevor's mother that they watched angry DI's take him away. A short time later, Trevor was admitted to the base mental clinic, suffering from "paranoid delusions." While being treated there, he was left unattended on a balcony from which he tragically fell or jumped. Paralyzed, he died about a month later. The family's lawyer, who had military experience with accident reports, criticized the Army's investigation as grossly inadequate.

Trevor's mother is bitter. "I had him for eighteen years," she told one Army officer, "and you had him for five days. You're going to be responsible for the rest of your lives."

There are two specific things that you can do before you leave home to prepare yourself for basic training. One is to work yourself into physical shape so that you can pass the initial strength tests and meet the military's standards for weight.

All of the services (except the Air Force) require that entering recruits be able to perform a certain number of exercises (see page 40). If you can't qualify, you'll be placed in a special "rehab" unit, and it may take you longer to get through basic. The second thing to do in preparation is to quit smoking. None of the services allows their recruits to smoke at any time during the entire training period. You don't want to suffer the effects of nicotine withdrawal during this stressful period.

BASIC TRAINING SITES

Army

The Army doesn't necessarily assign its recruits to the training base nearest their home. Under its "One Station Unit Training" concept, recruits usually take basic at the same base where they'll do their advanced training. Women recruits are trained only at the bases marked with asterisks. The length of basic is eight weeks. There were 100,000 trainees in 1988.

*Fort Dix, NJ	Fort Knox, KY	Fort Sill, OK
*Fort Jackson, SC	Fort Benning, GA	Fort Bliss, TX
*Fort McClellan, AL	Fort Leonard Wood, MO	

Note: Basic training will end at Fort Dix, NJ by Fall, 1991.

Navy

This branch also tries to match a sailor's basic training location to where he will undergo advanced training. Women recruits are trained only at the base marked with an asterisk. The length of basic is eight weeks. There were 100,000 trainees in 1988.

*Orlando, FL
Great Lakes, IL   (near Chicago)
San Diego, CA

Marines

Women recruits are trained only at the base marked with an asterisk. The length of basic is thirteen weeks for males, nine weeks for females. There were 35,500 trainees in 1988.

*Parris Island, SC (all recruits from east of the Mississippi)
San Diego, CA (all male recruits from the western United States)

Air Force

The length of basic is six weeks. There were 58,500 trainees in 1987. The barracks are air-conditioned due to extremely hot weather four to five months out of the year.

*Lackland AFB, near San Antonio, TX

Coast Guard

The length of basic is eight weeks. There were 5,100 trainees in 1988.

*Cape May, NJ

LEAVING FOR BASIC

Normally you will report to the same MEPS where you were initially screened. After you arrive (usually in the morning), you'll be given another physical to make sure you haven't developed new problems or gained or lost too much weight. Assuming that your health is still okay, you will be sent to the ceremony room to take the oath that will place you on active duty and subject you to the Uniform Code of Military Justice. From this moment until you are discharged, you're bound by the military's code of conduct, which is generally more strict than what you have been used to as a civilian (see Chapter 5).

MEPS personnel will have arranged for you to travel that day, by plane, bus, or train, to your assigned training post. You will most likely be traveling with other recruits, one of whom may be designated as an informal leader for the group. Remember, you are now on active duty and are subject to military law. Sometimes military policemen check out airport bars and lounges, looking for underage military personnel who are drinking illegally.

When you report to the MEPS, you should bring only the following items in a small gym bag: Social Security card; marriage or divorce papers and college transcripts (if applicable); shaving cream and razors; prescription glasses; one change of underwear and socks (females can bring additional clothing items such as bras, panties, and nightshirts); and no more than $25 in cash. You can purchase toiletry items at the base exchange.

You should *not* bring any of the following: jewelry, except for a small religious medal, engagement or wedding ring, and conventional watch; drugs or medicines, except prescription drugs; alcohol; dice; playing cards; radios; suitcases; books; tape recorders; pornography; or any kind of food, gum, or candy.

The Reception Center

Depending on the time you arrive at your basic training site, you
may either begin administrative processing or be fed and sent to
the center's dormitory for what's left of the night. The strict regimen of basic doesn't usually begin until recruits are sent to their
training units. The Marines, however, who like to be different,
have their recruits line up on yellow painted footprints as soon as
they get off the bus, and drill instructors impose strict discipline
no matter what the hour. You can expect a sleepless first night at
either Parris Island or San Diego, because the Marines don't allow their recruits to go to bed until they have completed preliminary processing, which includes receiving their uniforms.

The Air Force also assigns their recruits to their training units
shortly after they arrive and imposes a training regimen
immediately.

The "Amnesty Box"

In the Army, Air Force, Navy, and Coast Guard you will be given
an "amnesty briefing" shortly after you arrive. If you have
any contraband (drugs, weapons, alcohol, etc.), you will be allowed to go into an "amnesty booth," close the curtain, and toss
any such items into a locked box—no questions asked. Note,
however, that the Marines have no such program. If you're
caught with illegal items, you can be discharged at the discretion
of the commander.

Drugs and Alcohol Testing

Within three days after arrival at boot camp, all recruits must
furnish urine samples that are tested for residues from THC
(marijuana or hashish) and cocaine. A third test, which randomly
checks for either opiates, amphetamines, or PCP ("angel dust"),
was recently added. These residues, which scientists call metabolites, have been known to remain in the urine for thirty days or
more after use. Note that the Marines conduct these drug tests at
the MEPS.

If your urine sample registers positive, you can be discharged,
although the Navy doesn't automatically expel recruits whom it
thinks can be rehabilitated.

In 1988, the Army discharged 4,100 out of 100,000 (4.1 percent) new recruits for positive drug tests. The Navy expelled almost the same percentage, while the Marines sent 2.6 percent of enlistees home for this reason. The Air Force had the lowest rate discharging just over 1 percent for drug use. If you are discharged for marijuana use based on this test, you can reapply for enlistment after six months. If cocaine is detected, a year's wait is required.

You may wonder whether being forced to surrender your body's fluids violates your Constitutional rights against self-incrimination and arbitrary searches. A number of civil liberties groups and labor unions have asked the same question. However, courts have ruled that the military can legally impose these tests. Civilian employees, in contrast, have won some protection against compulsory testing.

You also will be required to take a breathalyzer test that measures the amount of alcohol in your system. A reading of .05 alcohol is enough to bar you from entering the military. The legal standard for intoxication in most states is set at twice the level, so watch your pre-boot camp celebrations! The number of GI's from all branches of the armed forces who flunk this test is very small; about one in a thousand. They can reapply after a six-month waiting period.

Pregnancy Test

All female recruits are tested. Those found to be pregnant will be discharged. It is possible to reapply for enlistment after the baby is born.

Physical Ability (Initial Strength Testing) and Weight Limits

Each of the services requires that both male and female recruits be able to perform a certain number of calisthenics upon entering the military. Each recruit's weight must also fall within limits relative to his height. The exercise requirements vary somewhat according to service branch and are scaled according to a recruit's sex and age. The following lists, by service, the current (March 1989) entrance requirements.

Army

Male recruits:
  8 to 13 consecutive push-ups, depending on age

Female recruits:
  1 push-up

Navy

Male recruits:
10 push-ups
25 jumping jacks
15 sit-ups, knees bent
10 flutter kicks
10 bodybuilders
(8-count squat thrust)
Run for 10 minutes, no
  distance required
Swimming—tread water for
  5 minutes, then swim 50
  yards within 5 minutes

Female recruits:
10 modified push-ups,
  kneeling position
25 jumping jacks
15 sit-ups, knees bent
10 flutter kicks
10 mountainclimbers
(2 count leg exercise)
Run for 10 minutes, no
  distance required
Swimming— tread water for
5 minutes, then swim 50
  yards within 5 minutes

Marines

Male recruits:
1 pull-up
35 sit-ups
1 1/2-mile run in less than
  13.31 minutes

Female recruits:
1 flexed-arm hang for 12
  seconds within a minute
19 sit-ups
3/4-mile run in less than 8.3
  minutes

Air Force

Has no entry-level physical requirements

Coast Guard

Male recruits:
20 push-ups
40 sit-ups
1 1/2-mile run in no more
  than 12 minutes
Swim 100 meters within 5
  minutes, then tread water
  for remainder of
  time.

Female recruits:
15 push-ups (modified-
  kneeling position)
40 sit-ups
1 1/2-mile run in no more
  than 13 minutes
Swim 100 meters within 5
minutes, then tread water
for remainder of time.

In order to graduate from basic, recruits generally must perform a number of exercises. The requirements are more difficult than the entrance standards.

Each of the services has set up rehab programs for recruits who aren't up to par, but the Army's Fitness Training Units (FTU) are probably the most extensive. They were created in 1985 to help stem the loss of recruits who were otherwise qualified. FTU's, which some GI's have dubbed "fat farms," have been set up at each basic training post. In 1988, over 7,000 soldiers participated in at least one phase of the three-week program, with over 90 percent eventually qualifying.

While assigned to a rehab unit, recruits work intensively on physical conditioning. They also receive instruction in nutrition, diet, and aerobics, as well as some limited military training. The Army tests them after a week, and those who pass the push-up test are then assigned to regular training units. Those who don't pass continue the exercise regimen and are retested at the end of the second and third weeks. The Marines sometimes keep out-of-shape recruits in their rehab unit for up to forty-five days. Time spent in the rehab unit may be added to the normal period of basic training.

TYPICAL SCHEDULE FOR RECEPTION CENTER (ARMY)

All of the services put their recruits through entrance processing, although the schedule and duration may vary from the sample given below. As a rule, recruits will march from one office to another. Much of the information is presented on videotaped television programs.

First Day

- Commander/1st Sergeant's welcome (usually videotaped).

- Haircut (males only, close-cut; it will cost you $3.50).

- Receive advance on pay (regular pay begins in two weeks).

- Immunologic shots.

- HIV-antibody (AIDS) blood test. If your blood is "positive" meaning that it contains antibodies to the AIDS virus, you'll be counseled and then processed for discharge.

- Issue of uniform and equipment. Only battle-dress uniforms (BDU's)—camouflaged fatigues—are issued. Dress uniforms are issued after the fifth week.

- Visit PX to purchase personal items: shoe and brass polish, soap, etc.

Second Day

- Briefing on personal affairs.

- "Moment of truth" briefing. Last chance to reveal, without punishment, problems that the recruit may have concealed from recruiters, such as a criminal conviction.

- Personnel records processing (pay, tax deductions, insurance, etc.).

- Issuance of ID cards, dog tags, family ID cards.

- Briefing on GI Bill (college assistance), after which recruits choose whether or not to participate. GI's who elect to participate will have $100 deducted from pay for twelve months. This deduction will not be refunded if a veteran later decides against college.

- Eye screening (glasses will be prescribed as needed).

- Dental screening (including X-rays).

Third Day

- Physical testing and weigh-in (must do minimum number of exercises; failures are sent to the "fat farms").

- Haircuts (for females only; hair cannot touch collar).

- Briefing on military law and Uniform Code of Military Justice.

- Briefing by chaplain on stress during training. Recruits may request private counseling with chaplain during basic.

- Protection of hearing (includes issuance of ear plugs).

- Aptitude testing. The Marines give all recruits a portion of the AS-VAB test again to ensure that their original scores reflect recruits' true abilities.

- Briefing on prevention of AIDS and other sexually transmitted diseases.

Usually, recruits are sent to their permanent training units on about the fourth day. Each service's basic is organized so that recruits are as isolated from civilian life as possible. This means that no visitors or phone calls are allowed, except by special permission. If an emergency occurs back home, your family should call the local Red Cross office, which will contact their counselors who work with the armed forces. If the Red Cross confirms that a serious problem exists with an immediate member of your family (spouse, child, parent, brother, or sister), you will be contacted, and special leave may be authorized.

TEN HUT! LIFE IN A TRAINING UNIT

The Navy, Marines, Air Force, Coast Guard, and some Army units house their recruits in open-bay barracks. Each training unit, which consists of roughly 60 recruits (up to 85 in the Navy), spends 24 hours a day together, sharing a large common room. Military educators believe that living this way helps mold individual recruits into a team that can work together, one of the primary goals of training.

Female recruits are housed together in similar, but separate barracks. Fraternization between the sexes during training is forbidden. Incidentally, the Army assigns male and female drill instructors to training platoons without regard to whether they are male or female units.

Some Army training posts, such as Fort Dix, NJ, have constructed barracks where recruits live eight to a room, but this remains the exception.

A Word About Drill Instructors

Like recruiting duty, being a drill instructor is not a job for which many GI's volunteer, although the Marines state that 80 percent of its DI's are volunteers. Even though a successful hitch in either job is considered a strong plus on a service record, the jobs can be highly stressful.

In most branches, DI's serve a minimum of two years, with a voluntary extension for a third (and final) year. About one third of the Army's DI's extend. As with recruiters, most DI's have served about seven years already and are planning to "do twenty" to earn their lifetime pension.

Drill instructors undergo a vigorous training program, which one DI called, "another boot camp within boot camp." Along with leadership training, drill and ceremony, and physical conditioning, instructors also learn about stress management and suicide prevention. The military tries to screen out candidates who are emotionally unsuited for the amount of control that instructors are given over recruits.

DI's no longer teach recruits the kind of soldiering skills that they once did. Today, they lead their charges from one specialist to another for training in various subjects.

Being a drill instructor is considered a tough, but rewarding job. The DI's I spoke to mentioned the "brutal" hours, beginning at 3:30 a.m. and extending into the evening, as the worst feature of the job. They receive up to $275 extra pay each month to partially compensate them for their time. DI's display a distinct *esprit de corps* (pride) in being "on the trail," as instructing is called in the Army.

A TYPICAL DAY OF BASIC TRAINING

Army

- Reveille (wake up) at 4:00-4:30 a.m.

- Wash, shave (no showering), make bed, clean personal area.

- Formation in front of barracks, march to chow.

- March back to barracks, change into gym clothes and running shoes.

- Physical training (PT) for 30 to 60 minutes. Instructor leads a variety of exercises: bend and reach; high jumps; turn and bounce; squat thrust; and the old favorite, push-ups. Every muscle group receives attention. PT may end with a march.

- Return to barracks for additional cleanup and preparation for daily inspection by the 1st Sergeant (approximately 6:30 a.m.)

- March to classroom for instruction in variety of military subjects such as first aid, rank system, and wearing of the uniform.

- March to lunch.

- Formation for Drill and Ceremonies training (marching, close-order drill to commands). The Army and the Marines spend a lot of time on this, devoting a hundred training hours to it. The other services give it less time and importance.

- March to classrooms for more instruction.
- Return to physical training area for more exercise.
- March to dinner.
- Return to barracks for additional cleaning and preparing for the next day's inspection. Study course materials, clean weapons, etc.
- Lights out at 9:00 p.m., unless DI is unhappy with unit's performance. Then unit may be required to do additional cleaning or drilling.

On Saturdays, the schedule remains pretty much the same, except for the weekly inspection in the ranks, followed by a full schedule of physical training and barracks maintenance. On Sundays, recruits get up an hour later than usual and can attend religious services in the base churches. After this, they perform more maintenance work during the afternoon. Some free time is allowed in the evening, but is restricted to on-base recreational facilities, assuming that the DI is satisfied with your unit's performance.

Marines (taken from actual time schedule)

5:00 a.m.	Reveille (wake up).
5:00-6:30	Breakfast, clean up barracks.
7:00-7:50	Haircuts.
8:00-9:20	Disassembly/assembly of M-16 rifle.
9:30-10:30	Care/cleaning of M-16 rifle.
11:30-12:20 p.m.	Noon meal (march to chow hall and back).
12:30-2:20	Close-order drill (precision marching/movements).
2:30-2:50	Physical stretching.
3:00-5:00	Physical training (exercises, calisthenics, running).
5:00-7:00	Dinner and commander's time (various activities under DI's supervision, such as cleaning, and polishing).
7:25-7:50	Drill instructor's hygiene inspection.
7:50-8:50	Free time, unless DI cancels for poor performance. You cannot leave the barracks area.
8:50-9:00	Final muster/devotions.
9:00	Taps (lights out).

The Marine Corps has issued a set of instructions, which provide that each recruit shall have the right to:

- Eight hours of uninterrupted sleep (this can be reduced to seven or six hours by order of the commander, for a good reason).

- One hour free time daily (can also be canceled as punishment).

- At least twenty minutes to eat each meal.

- Attend sick call as needed.

- Attend regularly scheduled religious services

- "Request mast" to present grievance to commander.

- Make and receive emergency phone calls.

- Receive mail as it arrives.

- Use the bathroom.

- Use medicine prescribed by Marine doctors.

- Have visitors (subject to restrictions).

Navy

5:30 a.m.	Reveille.
5:30-7:20	Barracks, cleanup, breakfast.
7:20-8:00	Training Period 1. Classes involve academic instruction on Navy subjects, training, and administrative activities. Examples are: basic deck seamanship; chemical/biological/radiological warfare-defense; chain of command; decision-making and time management; leave; liberty and conduct ashore; Navy mission; security; military drill.
8:10-8:50	Training Period 2.
9:00-9:40	Training Period 3.
9:50-10:30	Training Period 4.
10:40-11:20	Training Period 5.
11:20-1:00 p.m.	Lunch.
1:00-1:40	Training Period 6. (Physical conditioning and personal hygiene are each taught as one of these periods).
1:50-2:30	Training Period 7.
2:40-3:20	Training Period 8.
3:30-4:10	Training Period 9.

4:20-5:00	Training Period 10.
5:00	Evening meal.
6:30-7:30	All recruits shower and shine shoes.
7:30-8:15	All recruits on cleaning stations, clean barracks.
8:15-9:10	Study period and letter writing.
9:10-9:25	Instructions by NCO and night bunk check.
9:25-9:30	Tattoo (preparation for lights out).
9:30 p.m.	Taps (lights out).

All of the services regularly assign their recruits to extra work details such as KP (kitchen police), cleanup crews, or guard duty during basic. The Navy, for example, assigns its recruits to two-hour stints of watchstanding almost from the time training begins. This includes guard duty, sentry duty, fire watches, and barracks watches. Its recruits are required to memorize a complicated list of rules governing watchstanding that the Navy calls the "General Orders."

As you can see from these schedules, basic training is highly regimented, with everything planned down to the last second. In fact, the military intentionally doesn't allow enough time to perform some tasks, so that recruits will learn to manage their time more carefully. At Fort Dix, for instance, there are only six sinks for sixty recruits, forcing them to develop a system whereby everyone can get at least minimal sink time.

SYNOPSIS OF EIGHT-WEEK TRAINING CYCLE (ARMY)

The training schedules for the other branches are similar to this, although each varies its course material to reflect its individual mission.

First Week

After recruits complete initial processing at the Reception Center, they are assigned to their permanent training units. During the rest of this week, recruits are introduced to the fundamentals of military life. This includes instruction on the military's rank system and customs, such as saluting, wearing of the uniform, and basic commands. They also learn about standard operating procedures (SOP's) for sick call, meals, requesting leave, mail, use of the PX, etc. Extensive physical training and drill and ceremonies (close-order drill) begin.

Second Week

Recruits continue the daily regimen of physical exercise and drill and ceremonies. They receive instruction in drug and alcohol abuse as well as hands-on first-aid training in such techniques as mouth-to-mouth resuscitation and bandaging wounds. Lectures are given on the military justice system, including court-martials and the system of nonjudicial punishment (Article 15). Recruits are introduced to the M-16 rifle, the basic infantry weapon. Other weapons, including the M-60 machine gun, light antitank weapon (LAW), hand grenades, and the Claymore mine also are demonstrated.

In addition, recruits are trained in the use of the gas mask as a defense against chemical warfare. To generate realism, recruits don their masks and enter a special gas chamber. After gas is released, they must remove the mask and state their name, rank, and number before exiting.

Third Week

The principal activity of the next two weeks is the training of all recruits (both male and female) to "qualify" on the target range with the M-16 rifle. Like the Marines, the Army considers this to be one of the most important objectives of basic. They each devote over 100 training hours to it. Training on the M-16 stresses four fundamentals: steady position for firing; proper aiming point for sights; breath control; and steady trigger squeeze.

Students practice first with a computerized machine called the "Weaponeer" that electronically simulates actual rifle fire. From studying the shot pattern on the machine's target printout, students learn how to properly align the rifle's sights and to correct errors in their aiming.

The Marines put their recruits "on the grass" for an entire week, where they are taught everything about the rifle before they actually fire it. The Marines only use the "Weaponeer" as a remedial device with deficient shooters.

During the first four days of this training, the Army recruits bivouac in tents near the rifle range. While encamped, they also are taught weapons safety and maintenance.

Fourth Week

M-16 training continues, and about mid-week, students fire live ammunition for the first time. After studying their targets, firing range instructors offer each recruit corrective advice. Following additional target shooting, recruits are put through a "dry run" of the qualification test.

On qualifying day, a recruit must score at least 23 out of 40 possible target points. Probably because this training is so intensive, over 90 percent of recruits in both the Army and the Marines pass on their first try. Those who fail are given some remedial training and then tested again, on the same day. Those who fail a second time return for additional training and are retested the following week.

During this week, recruits also handle and in some cases fire other weapons, such as the M-60 machine gun, LAW, and the Claymore mine. Physical conditioning and drilling continues on a daily basis. At week's end, recruits are allowed to go to the base gym, swimming pool, and snack bar.

Fifth Week

A tactical bivouac is this week's highlight. During basic, recruits complete marches of 5, 10, and 15 miles while carrying combat gear. The Marines do a similar amount of distance marching. Both male and female recruits march, with rifle and pack, to a remote site where they pitch tents for a four-night encampment under simulated combat conditions. They dine on meals-ready-to-eat (MRE's), a freeze-dried delicacy that has been compared unfavorably to C rations. During this bivouac, recruits are taught how to construct simple defensive positions such as trenches and foxholes and to engage in active patrolling day and night. Recruits also are trained in the use of hand grenades by throwing as many as twelve "practice" grenades at targets fifty and more meters distant. Recruits are then tested on the Hand Grenade Assault Course, which requires the throwing of two live grenades.

Sixth Week

Recruits are taken to the Infiltration Course, which is designed to simulate some of the obstacles (trenches, tree stumps, abandoned equipment, barbed wire, etc.) that GI's might encounter on an actual battlefield. With its rope climb, cargo nets, and other challenges, this course primarily tests the physical endurance of each recruit. After orientation, recruits often go through the course at night.

GI's also return to the rifle range for training on firing at moving targets. Recruits are given Sunday afternoon off, but they are restricted to base facilities.

Seventh Week

Drill and ceremonies is performed for inspection. Recruits return to the rifle range, this time to learn to fire the M-16 rifle while moving on combat assaults.

GI's are briefed on the Confidence Course. This consists of scaling high walls, swinging on ropes, jumping from towers, and circumventing obstacles such as pits and trenches. This is designed to build each individual recruits confidence in himself and the team. It teaches trust and dependence on others. All recruits take the physical qualification test. Male recruits (age 17-21) must do 42 push-ups within two minutes, 52 sit-ups within two minutes, and a 2 mile run in less than fifteen minutes and 54 seconds.

Female recruits (age 17-21) are required to do 18 push-ups within two minutes, 50 sit-ups within two minutes, and run 2 miles in less than 18 minutes and 54 seconds.

Older recruits are required to meet slightly less stringent exercise standards.

Eighth Week

All recruits must take and pass the End-of-Cycle Test. This is a hands-on test in which each recruit must perform satisfactorily twenty different tasks at four different stations:

First Station—First Aid

1. Treat patient for shock.
2. Splint a fracture.

3. Evaluate a casualty.

4. Apply field dressing.

5. Remove object from throat.

6. Perform mouth-to-mouth resuscitation.

Second Station—Nuclear, Biological, and Chemical Weapons

1. Evaluate chemical situation.

2. Demonstrate proper use of gas mask.

Third Station—U.S. Weapons

1. Prepare, fire, and recover a Claymore mine.

2. Adjust sights on M-16 by studying shot-group pattern.

3. Put shoulder-fired light antitank weapon (LAW) into operation.

Fourth Station—Movement of Unit under Fire

1. Demonstrate map-reading ability.

2. Find position using compass.

3. Order movement of unit under simulated direct fire.

After this all-day test is completed, recruits begin their out-processing from basic (records, finances, and duty orders for next assignment), and turn in organization equipment. They prepare for graduation with a winding down of routine.

The last step in basic training is the graduation ceremony. Say "cheese!"

A Special Note on Marine Basic Training

Traditionally, the Marines have operated as a lightly armed, highly mobile, amphibious fighting force. Their slogan "every Marine a rifleman" conveys the idea of a lean strike force having little fat or bureaucracy. Marines pride themselves on being different from the Army, which they consider to be top-heavy with paper-pushers and armchair commanders.

Of course, the reality is a bit more complicated. Although the Marines can field a higher ratio of fighters to support personnel than the Army (its "tooth-to-tail ratio"), a sizeable administrative support structure has evolved in the Corps, as well.

In recent years, a number of Marine leaders, including the current Commandant, Gen. A.M. Grey, have decided that the Corps has strayed away from military fundamentals and that its ability to fight has been compromised by thickening layers of bureaucracy.

The Commandant issued a "White Letter" memo to all Marines in October 1988, defining the new training goal as follows: "All hands must be capable of effectively serving in a rifle squad on combat operations. . . . Every Marine, regardless of occupational specialty [job] will be taught those fundamental skills needed to survive and fight on today's battlefield."

The net effect of this policy change for male Marine recruits is that they must undergo an additional four weeks of "advanced" combat training. After graduation from basic at either Parris Island or San Diego, male recruits are given ten days off, and then sent to a new School of Infantry at either Camp LeJeuene, NC, or Camp Pendleton, CA.

There, they will spend four weeks undergoing infantry training in the following areas:

- Complete field firing course with M-16 (both offensive and defensive tactics).

- Training in use of crew-served M-2 and MK-19 machine guns (maintenance, emplacement, sighting, and firing).

- Training in small-unit combat leadership (including "four characteristics that allow Marines to overcome fear").

- Close combat (bayonet and hand-to-hand Level II).

- 15-mile forced march with full gear (in less than 5 hours).

- Combat conditioning course (rope climb, 30 push-ups, evacuate an "injured" person 50 yards, advance by fire, 3-mile run.)

- Intelligence collection, analysis, and reporting.

- Training on Warsaw Pact tactics and "low intensity combat" (for example, El Salvador).

- Training in motorized operations.

- Defensive measures against air attacks.

- Construction of defensive emplacements (900 sand bags used by small unit).

- Booby-trap and mine detection.

QUITTING BASIC

No one is likely to report to basic unless he intends to finish it. Sometimes, however, despite their best intentions, people just cannot handle it, either physically, psychologically, or both. In the interest of fair disclosure, I confess that I could barely tolerate two weeks of Boy Scout camp!

Seriously, if you become totally depressed and miserable during basic, you should consider quitting, rather than risking injury or worse. As I explained, if the DI's identify you as a "wimp" or a "quitter," you can be singled out for some very unpleasant harassment. But there are greater dangers in training that must also be considered.

The Congressional study of Navy training deaths mentioned on page 32 concluded that the command often didn't conduct proper investigations of deaths or take corrective action. Less than two years before recruit Mirecki drowned, another sailor had to be hospitalized after nearly drowning under similar circumstances. Only after Mirecki's tragic death generated a storm of unfavorable publicity did the Navy begin to clean up its act.

If you decide to quit, you must first submit your request to your immediate superior, your drill instructor. He will probably do one of three things; harass you even more, ignore your request, or try to talk you out of it. Next, you should ask to see the chaplain. Again, chaplains are regular military officers, and part of their job is to persuade reluctant recruits to stick it out.

The Navy recently (June 1989) announced a new policy that I think may have dangerous consequences. In an effort to reduce recruit failure, no one will be allowed to quit basic during the first three weeks, even if they have medical problems. This could lead to tragedy for recruits who are totally unsuited for Navy life. For example, training commands are now under orders to keep even sailors who make "manipulative suicide gestures."

The Navy and Marines give recruits the right to "request mast," a procedure that allows them to present grievances to a superior officer. The outcome of such a request, however, will depend largely on the policies and preferences of each training commander.

In general, the commander has the authority to send home any recruit whom he feels, "lacks the proper attitude, aptitude, or motivation," to succeed in the military. Recruits who are separated during the first six months of service are usually given an "uncharacterized" general discharge. This is a notch below an "honorable" discharge.

The fact is, it won't be easy to leave the military during basic training. However, it may be better to put yourself through the hassle than to risk injury or worse. Sometimes, recruits who try to stick it out only land in more trouble. If you are charged with a military crime such as disobedience, you could end up with a bad conduct discharge as well as some jail time.

Persons who are discharged during training will have a "reenlistment code" placed on their military discharge form (DD214). A code of either "RE-1" or "RE-2" means that the veteran is eligible to reenlist in the future. However, if you receive an "RE-3" code, you cannot rejoin without special permission from the district recruiting command. An "RE-4" code constitutes a permanent bar to reenlistment.

In the aftermath of Navy recruit Mirecki's drowning, the Navy established a Training Performance Evaluation Board composed of fifteen officers to monitor high-risk training in the future.

The Congressional study of Navy training deaths proposed a number of additional reforms that I believe should be adopted by all the service branches. They are as follows:

1. Give all recruits the right to quit any training activity that they find too frightening or difficult.

2. Protect such recruits from any sanction or penalty because of their decision to quit.

3. Insure that enlistment contracts spell out clearly just what kind of training will be required for specific jobs.

4. Follow up with recruits who quit programs to learn what they objected to.

5. Improve the screening process for military instructors.

6. Develop psychological screening programs for recruits who are scheduled to undergo training in any of the 109 Navy courses that involve some risk of physical harm.

A POSTSCRIPT

Shortly after Congress and the Navy completed their extensive reviews of training practices, another young sailor, Michael Fedie, aged twenty-two, of Altoona, WI, died unexpectedly at the Pensacola, FL, facility on June 23, 1989. Fedie had jumped from a twelve foot tower into a swimming pool as part of an abandon-ship exercise. Wearing flight gear, he swam fifteen yards before collapsing as he climbed from the pool. A military autopsy was unable to determine the exact cause of death.

Chapter 3

Advanced Skills Training

In recent years, vocational training has become more important to the military for two reasons. First, recruits have been led to expect to receive skills training as part of the enlistment bargain. Second, the sophisticated equipment and weapons used by the armed forces today require GI's to have more technical skills than in the past.

A current television commercial for the Army urges young people to "get an edge on life" by joining up. The ad shows a rough-and-ready combat soldier dissolving into a briefcase-toting businessman. A recent Pentagon survey found that half of its recruits today listed "job experience and training" as their primary motive for enlisting.

Taken as a whole, the armed forces today offer about 2,000 different skills-training courses. You should remember two things about this training: it is often quite superficial, and it often trains you on specialized equipment that is used only by the military.

The official Military Career Guide for 1988-89 states that most of its advanced training courses run from 10 to 20 weeks. My impression is that the majority are closer to the lower figure. The average length of the Army's nearly 500 different skills courses is between 9 and 10 weeks (55 days of instruction). Obviously, this is not enough time to provide much more than a basic orientation to complicated technical subjects.

For example, carpenters and bricklayers in the military are trained for five to eight weeks at a technical school, depending on the service branch. By comparison, union apprentices in these skill areas in civilian life undergo several years of classroom and on-the-job training before they achieve journeyman status. Private vocational schools, which will be discussed later, require a year's intensive training for these kinds of jobs.

The military justifies the relatively brief school programs by noting that a GI will continue to receive "on-the-job" and other advanced training throughout his military career. However, once you are assigned to your permanent unit, there is no guarantee that such training will continue. If your commander is short-handed and needs you to perform an essential, but undemanding job, he may not be willing to permit you time off for advanced training. Once you are in a regular unit, whether or not your training continues will depend greatly on the command's workload and other factors outside of your control.

Because its primary purpose is to wage war, the military has many jobs such as tank crew member, graves registration, or explosives-disposal specialist, for which there is no civilian equivalent. The case of a recently discharged Army veteran, Gerald H. from Michigan, illustrates this problem. Gerald enlisted hoping to receive technical training. He was sent for a six-week training course on the Lance missile at Fort Sill's artillery school. According to Gerald, the training centered on the mechanics of the Lance missile. His class never actually trained with the weapon. As luck would have it, the missle unit to which he was assigned in West Germany was commanded by the British military. As a result, Gerald spent his two years there on guard duty. He sums up his three-year hitch as "a total waste."

To add to the confusion, some military job titles are misleading. An "indirect fire specialist," for instance, is the Army's new name for someone who lugs and fires a mortar tube.

The military also has many other jobs that fall into a "grey area." Some veterans will be able to transfer these skills to civilian jobs; others will not. For instance, the Navy and Coast Guard combined have 95,000 people who work as seamen. Only a small fraction of these people can expect to find similar work aboard civilian ships.

Many of the military's skills courses don't last long enough to provide more than a general introduction to technical subjects. An instructor at the Army's light-truck mechanics school at Fort Dix observed, "You can only cover so much material, given the time we have to work with. Only about three out of ten students here will ever become real truck mechanics," he predicted. "Some of them don't even want to be here."

The training commanders also face a problem that is not of their own making: the declining academic skills of entering recruits. At least 22,500 out of 90,000 Navy recruits who are tested annually cannot pass a ninth-grade reading comprehension test, according to the *Navy Times*. Because most Navy technical manuals are written for the tenth-grade level or higher, this creates some real problems. Even this level of reading may be below business standards. According to the President of the Business Council for Effective Literacy, "most jobs today require skills approaching twelfth-grade levels."

A teacher at the Navy's torpedo-mates school in Orlando recently told the *Tampa Tribune*, "We teach at a sixth-grade level, and we still have kids [who] have to be spoon-fed through the course."

Some educators argue that the military has watered down the quality of some of its technical courses as a means of coping with their recruits' deficiencies. Instead of teaching scientific theory, these critics argue, the armed services have adopted a simplistic "by-the-numbers" approach. This may enable graduates to get by in certain jobs, but they won't understand the underlying principles and concepts.

Tech. Sgt. David Denman, who teaches a radar course at Keesler AFB, described the problem to the *Tampa Tribune*: "I ask [students] to tell me how radar works and they give me canned responses. They don't grasp how it all comes together." He also explained how many technicians solve problems today: "You get it [a problem] down to the ballpark, then you replace the whole ballpark."

If you are considering the military primarily because you want skills training, you owe it to yourself to check out other alternatives as well. There are thousands of private vocational schools throughout the United States that offer a wide range of skills-training courses. Because these schools depend on their ability to place graduates in jobs as a means of attracting new students, they are very sensitive to the skills that employers want their new employees to have.

You should ask your high school counselors as well as friends for the names of schools in your community that have a good reputation. Over 1,200 vocational schools belong to the National Association of Trade and Technical Schools (NATTS), which requires its member-schools to maintain minimum educational standards. NATTS has an accrediting commission that regularly visits its member schools to monitor compliance with the group's professional standards. You may want to send for a free handbook that lists, by training subject, all NATTS schools in the United States. (Write: Handbook, Dept. KIT, P.O. Box 10429, Rockville, MD 20850.)

The average course of instruction at a NATTS-affiliated school today lasts forty weeks. Classes generally meet five hours a day, five days a week. Tuition ranges from $1,500 to $7,000, depending on the length of the course.

As a rule, the classroom phase of skills training in the military is much shorter. For instance, an X-ray technician in a private vocational school will undergo 100 weeks of instruction, compared with 12 to 19 weeks in a military program. The military's aircraft mechanics receive between 3 and 17 weeks of classroom training as opposed to 33 to 84 weeks in private schools. As noted, the military claims that its personnel receive continuous "on-the-job" training, but it may be a hit-or-miss thing. With private vocational schools, you know exactly how long you will be in training when you sign up.

Two vocational experts, Dr. James Myers and Elizabeth Scott used Labor Department statistics to compile a list of the fastest growing and declining occupations in their new book, *Getting Skilled, Getting Ahead* (Peterson's Guides, Princeton, NJ). Both lists appear below, although I have omitted jobs that are not found in the military.

Fastest Growing Occupations (1986-2000)	Percentage increase in total jobs by year 2000
Paralegal personnel	104%
Medical assistants	90
Physical therapists	88
Data processing equipment repairers	80
Computer systems analysts, electronic data processing	76
Medical records technicians	75
Computer programmers	70
Radiologic technicians	65
Dental hygienists/assistants	60
Electronic data processing operators	51
Data entry keyers, composing	51

Fastest Declining Occupations (1986-2000)	Percentage decrease in total jobs by year 2000
Electrical and electronic assemblers	54%
Electronic semiconductor processors	51
Industrial truck and tractor operators	34
Telephone station installers and repairers	32
Chemical equipment operators and tenders	30

Stenographers	28
Statistical clerks	26
Central office and PBX installers, telephone	23
Typesetters and compositors	17

These lists illustrate broad trends and may help you evaluate which career fields offer the most opportunities and which ones you should avoid.

By suggesting that you check out private vocational schools, I'm not implying that the military doesn't provide many GI's with valuable skills training, because it does. What you need to figure out is whether the military training you are promised will prepare you for a civilain job with a future.

MILITARY JOBS WITH A CIVILIAN FUTURE

Listed below are my choices for military jobs that will best prepare you for civilian employment. After the job listing, the total number of these positions in the entire military is given, followed by the number of new openings that occur in an average year. Titles are from the Military Career Guide. The various branches may use different names for the same job. Note that some of the most desirable jobs have relatively few openings each year. Remember that 250,000 new recruits now go on active duty annually.

- Radar and Sonar Maintenance (28,000 total jobs, 2,900 needed annually).

- Air Traffic Controllers (12,000 total jobs, 1,200 needed annually).

- Electronics Weapons and Electrical Machinery Maintenance (54,000 total jobs, 6,100 needed annually).

- Computer Programmers and Systems Analysts (7,100 total jobs, 750 needed annually). Note: An estimated 813,000 programmers will be working in the civilian economy by the year 2000. The military obviously trains only a tiny fraction of this total.

- Data Processing Maintenance (9,000 total jobs, 870 needed annually).

- Aircraft Mechanics (147,000 total jobs, 17,000 needed annually). This is the largest category of jobs. However, only those who are extensively trained will be able to cash in on the civilian job market. Line workers who perform semiskilled maintenance jobs like changing tires or washing planes cannot expect to be pursued by the civilian aviation industry.

- Foreign Language Interpreters and Translators (6,400 total jobs, 1,200 needed annually).

- Health Care (85,000 total jobs, 13,000 needed annually). This category covers a multitude of jobs: nurses (RN and LPN); physical therapists; pharmacy and medical records clerks: mental health workers; radiologic technicians; occupational therapists; diagnostic personnel; dental technicians; etc.

- Electronic Warfare/Radio Intelligence (25,000 total jobs, 3,000 needed annually). Several federal agencies, the CIA, FBI, and National Security Agency (NSA), hire veterans from this field.

- Military Police (68,000 total jobs, 14,000 needed annually).

- Fire Fighters (12,000 total jobs, 1,500 needed annually). Note, however, that a young person who is qualified can join a local police or fire department after high school and be trained at government expense. He will gain several years seniority over his buddies who join the military, seeking the same training.

- Power Plant Operators (25,000 total jobs, 2,500 needed annually). These people operate power plants using coal, oil, and nuclear fission. The Navy's Nuclear Field Program trains operators for its many nuclear ships and submarines. It is one of the longest courses offered by the military.

Military personnel who qualify for jobs that require extensive training, such as jet pilots, foreign language analysts, or the nuclear power field, must obligate themselves to additional years of service. Recruiters sometimes downplay the difficulty of these courses. It will be up to you to pass the proficiency tests. One young man who was recently victimized is Craig Higgins, of Newburgh, NY, whose case I was involved with in 1988. Craig was an average student in high school. He barely passed the one year of mathematics that he took. His score on the entrance exam for the Navy's Nuclear Field Program was just one point above passing. Nonetheless, his recruiter convinced Craig to enlist in the nuclear program, even though it requires a six-year service obligation. Higgins also claims that the recruiter told him that he could later earn $60,000 a year in the civilian nuclear power industry.

Despite Craig's best efforts, he could not keep up with the course work. Many of his fellow students had taken several years of math and physics in high school. After Craig was dropped from the nuclear school, he received another surprise—he would have to serve the full six years, although now as a maintenance crewmember aboard an oiler. After unsuccessfully requesting reassignment, Craig grew frustrated and went AWOL. After a few months, he contacted Citizen Soldier, a GI-rights advocacy organization, and we arranged for civilian counsel and Craig's return to military custody. He was court-martialed, given brig time, and sent back to duty on the oiler.

Today, Craig is back home in Newburgh with an other-than-honorable discharge. He feels bitter about the Navy's treatment of him. "They just take people into that nuke program, let them wash out, and put them into the fleet," he charges. "I'm back where I started, just scraping for money to go to college." One recruiting official told reporters who inquired about Craig's treatment that as many as half of those who enter the Navy's nuclear program fail to graduate.

All military jobs for the enlisted ranks have been organized into an occupational classification system that consists of about 2,000 different military occupational specialties (MOS) used by all the service branches. These are divided into the following nine occupational areas:

1. *Infantry, gun crew, and seamanship specialists.* This classification includes armor and amphibious, combat engineering, artillery, rockets and missiles, air crews, and security personnel.

2. *Electronic equipment repairers.* This classification includes those who maintain and repair radio/radar, fire control, missile guidance, nuclear weapons equipment, teletype, and cryptographic (secret coding) equipment.

3. *Communications and intelligence specialists.* This classification includes radio and teletype operators; sonar, radar, and air traffic controllers; signal intelligence/electronic warfare; intelligence collection and analysis; and combat operations control.

4. *Medical and dental specialists.*

5. *Other technical and allied specialists.* This classification includes photography, mapping, surveying, weather forecasting, ordnance disposal, diving, nuclear, biological, and chemical (NBC) warfare, fire fighters, etc.

6. *Functional support and administration.* Examples are personnel, data processing, accounting and finance, clerical, public affairs, religious, and social service workers.

7. *Electrical/mechanical equipment repairers.* This classification includes those who repair aircraft engines, automotives, wire communications, shipboard propulsion, power-generating equipment, armament and munitions missile systems, precision equipment, etc.

8. *Craftsmen.* This classification includes metalworking, construction, plumbing, printing, tailoring, and industrial gas and fuel production.

9. *Service and supply.* This classification includes food service, motor transport, law enforcement, laundry and dry cleaning, and warehouse workers.

Martin Binkin, a military analyst from the Brookings Institute, has estimated that military jobs today are about evenly divided between blue-collar and white-collar occupations. Incidentally, jobs that consist of traditional military skills, such as infantrymen or naval guncrew members, have held steadily at about one out of six jobs for the past 30 years.

All of the service branches, except for the Marines, operate a vast array of training courses at military bases throughout the world. The Marine Corp economizes by sending most of its recruits to be trained as "guests" of the other branches' schools.

HOW ASSIGNMENTS ARE MADE

Training assignments occur in one of three ways. Some recruits have a formal promise of training written into their enlistment contract. For the record, the military's position is that the recruit is not bound by the contract if the military cannot deliver on its promise for some reason. In practice, however, some recruiters may tell recruits that they will have to pick a different skill field instead of being released from their commitment.

Some training assignments are made during basic, based on a recruit's performance. A third group of recruits is arbitrarily assigned to whatever schools have vacancies at any time after they sign their enlistment contract. As a rule, these will be the least desirable training slots.

TRAINING ENVIRONMENT

One thing that often surprises trainees, especially in the Army and Navy, is that the strict discipline of basic training is carried over into the advanced individual training (AIT) period. GI's enrolled in AIT courses at Fort Dix told me that their lives continued to be strictly regimented. Some people think that when basic is over, the pressure will ease, but this is often not the case. The students at Fort Dix continued to be awakened at dawn, put through daily physical exercises and regular inspections, and marched in formations to class. However, students were permitted some time off on Sundays, when they could go off base for a few hours.

The following is an excerpt of a letter I received from a Marine taking advanced training at a Naval base in Tennessee in October 1989: "Millington is very strict. Every day from 6 a.m. until 3 p.m., we are under close supervision of Marine Corps and Navy instructors. Inside the school building we are given ten-minute breaks each hour. We are denied the right to read anything other than school-related material. We mustn't talk in the passageways, and we must walk up against the bulkhead at all times. Weekends are fine. I can leave the base as often as I want."

A spokesperson for Air Force training programs stated that their skills-training programs also maintain a fairly high level of military discipline, although the environment was considerably "more relaxed" than during basic training.

I don't claim to be trained as an educator, but I can't help wondering if the fatigue and distractions that are an inevitable result of the strict discipline aren't counterproductive to learning. Most people learn best when they are rested, relaxed, and unstressed.

As a rule, the military's training programs use a mixture of classroom lecturers and demonstrations, video programs, and "hands-on" practical training.

Outlined below is a brief description of advanced training offered by each service branch after basic.

Army Advanced Training

The Army currently has 323 different Military Occupational Specialties (MOS's), of which 48 jobs are closed to female soldiers. They are organized into 32 Career Management Fields (CMF's). These are further broken down into three general categories: combat, combat support, and combat service support. The least desirable MOS's, in terms of civilian employment, have the lowest numbers, starting with "11" and going through "27." The more desirable MOS numbers begin with "29" and run through "98."

Under the Army's Single Unit Training concept, recruits take their basic at the same base where they'll receive their AIT, whenever possible. This is done to save travel time and expense. Listed below are the basic training bases paired with AIT schools.

Basic Training Site	State	Advanced Skills Taught
Fort Dix*	NJ	Light-wheel vehicle maintenance, food service, truck driving, fuel truck operator.
Fort Jackson	SC	Heavy and light vehicle maintenance, small-arms repair, personnel administration, food service, record keeping.
Fort McClellan	AL	Military police (law enforcement, corrections), nuclear, biological and chemical (NBC) weapons training.
Fort Knox	KY	Armor, tanks, personnel carriers, etc.
Fort Benning	GA	Advanced Infantry training, Airborne and Rangers Schools. Airborne lasts three weeks and requires five parachute jumps. Ranger school lasts 58 consecu-

---

*Basic training is slated to end by Fall, 1991 and advanced training will be transferred to other bases by Fall, 1992.

tive days and is very arduous (one meal a day) and physically very stressful.

Fort Leonard Wood	MO	Combat engineers, heavy equipment operation, construction, typography, etc.
Fort Sill	OK	Field artillery, howitzers, light and heavy missiles with conventional and nuclear warheads.
Fort Bliss	TX	Air Defense Systems, short range air defense artillery, Nike, Hercules missile artillery, Hawk and Patriot missiles.

The following bases offer only advanced training courses; no basic is given:

Advanced Training Site	State	Advanced Skills Taught
Fort Devens	MA	Military intelligence specialties.
Fort Monmouth	NJ	Chaplain's School.
Fort Belvoir	VA	Engineer's School.
Aberdeen Proving Grounds	MD	Ordnance School, explosives and munitions research, testing and disposal.
Fort Lee	VA	Quartermaster School, supply and material management.
Fort Eustis	VA	Transportation School, motor/rail, marine, and terminal operations.
Charlottesville	VA	Judge Advocate General School, lawyers, judges, and legal workers.
Fort Bragg	NC	Special Warfare School, parachutists, and "Green Berets."
Fort Gordon	GA	Signal School, various types of communications/electronics/data processing training.
Fort Rucker	AL	Aviation School, helicopter flight and maintenance training.
Fort Sam Houston	TX	Health Sciences School.
Fort Huachuca	AZ	Military intelligence; tactical counterintelligence; signal,

imagery, electronic warfare, and cryptographic (coding) operations.

Presidio/Monterey   CA   Defense Language School (80% of graduates work in electronics/intelligence fields).

The Army, Navy, and Marine Corps all operate an apprenticeship program for certain skill areas, in conjunction with the federal Department of Labor. GI's who fulfill the requirements for instruction and supervised work (from 2,000 to 8,000 hours) are eligible to be certified as journeymen in their skill field. This credential may be valuable to some civilian employers.

Navy Advanced Training

The Navy offers two types of advanced training: its technical schools, which it calls "A" and "B" schools, and apprenticeship training. For enlisted personnel, the Navy divides its jobs (called "ratings") into twenty-four occupational career fields. Examples are ship maintenance, health care, and ship operations.

Currently, about three out of four Navy recruits receive advanced technical training after basic. About 60 percent of them are assigned to one of the sixty "A" schools, which teach the basic technical knowledge that sailors will need to perform their initial jobs. Course length varies from a few weeks to many months, depending on the subjects being studied. "A" school graduates later receive additional specialized training. A number of the "A" schools are clustered at the three basic training sites—Great Lakes, Orlando, and San Diego. The others are located at Memphis, TN, Gulfport, MS, Newport, RI, Pensacola, FL, Norfolk, VA, and Port Hueneme, CA.

Apprenticeship training is offered for jobs such as fireman, seaman, and airman. It typically lasts about four weeks.

Air Force Advanced Training

Since its primary mission is to service and operate technologically sophisticated aircraft and missiles, many Air Force courses are more lengthy than those of the other branches. The Air Force lists about 250 different jobs, 2 percent of which are currently closed to females. These are subdivided into about fifty "job areas," which are further divided into general skill (aptitude) areas. These four aptitude areas are listed below, followed by examples of jobs.

1. *Administrative.* Accounting, finance, cargo, and radio operator.

2. *Electronics.* Instrumentation systems, missile electronics, and computer and radar operator.

3. *General.* Medical corpsman, printer, and lab technician.

4. *Mechanical.* Welding, aircraft maintenance, carpentry, and aircraft system maintenance.

The following bases offer advanced training courses:

Advanced Training Site	State	Advanced Skills Taught
Lackland AFB	TX	Home of AF Basic, security police, pararescue, combat air controllers, recruiters school, social action/human relations, explosive ordnance, and cryptography (secret codes).
Sheppard AFB	TX	Health sciences, technical training in many subjects, statistical data processing and analysis, guided missiles, flight training; cable, antenna, and telephone maintenance.
Chanute AFB	IL	Weapons systems support, aircraft maintenance, electronics, and meteorology (weather).
Keesler AFB	MS	Offers 250 courses in computers, radar, avionics, intelligence, communications, personnel, and administration.
Lowry AFB	CO	Various technical schools, including supply and finance.

Incidentally, Air Force recruiting literature claims that 95 percent of its jobs are directly applicable to civilian jobs. Although this may be an exaggeration, overall, the Air Force does prepare more of its members for civilian jobs than the other branches.

Marines Advanced Training

The Corps divides work into 300 different MOS's in thirty-eight occupational fields. Because it is much smaller than the other branches (and technically a Navy subdivision), the Marines operate only a few of their own advanced training schools. Most of its trainees are sent to technical schools operated by the other branches, as follows.

- Military police (Air Force, Lackland AFB, TX).
- Armor (Army, Fort Knox, KY).
- Artillery (Army, Fort Sill, OK).
- Legal services (Navy, Newport, RI).
- Helicopter operations (Navy, Memphis, TN).
- Antitank defense (Army, Fort Bliss, TX).

While attending these schools, Marines maintain their identity in a special detachment, but participate as equals with students from other services.

Coast Guard Advanced Training

Unlike the other services, the Coast Guard sends its recruits directly to a Coast Guard unit for six months after they finish basic. The idea is that new people should acquire some practical experience with the Coast Guard before they make decisions about further training or job assignment. When the six months are over, most are sent to various "A" Schools that offer technical courses lasting anywhere from ten to forty-two weeks. These schools operate much like the Navy's "A" schools. "B" schools offer training in generalized subjects such as administration, leadership, or law enforcement. "C" schools provide more specialized training for different "rates" (jobs) for example, machinery technician, public affairs, or sonar technician.

Chapter 4

Life in the Military Today

"You're in the Army now,
You're not behind a plow,
You'll never get rich,
You son of a bitch,
You're in the Army now."

—TRADITIONAL SONG

Once upon a time, many young men joined the military to escape the harsh burdens of farm life or inner-city poverty. A coal miner in Virginia told me that in his town, a recruiter's best form of advertising was to display mess hall menus and woolen uniforms to attract the sons of impoverished coal miners.

Although there is probably as much poverty and homelessness in America today as at any time in its history, the military no longer offers much opportunity for our neediest citizens. Today's recruits still join in search of self-improvement; however, they come almost exclusively from working families, not the hardcore unemployed.

It used to be that a soldier or sailor could pretty much decide how long he would serve on active duty, provided that he showed up for work and stayed out of serious trouble. He did not have to prove he was physically fit twice a year, nor did he have to pass an annual test proving his job competence, as he does today. If some poundage crept onto his midsection, if he smoked or had a few drinks every night at the NCO (noncommissioned officers) Club, nobody much cared. Life in the military has changed.

The military today relies heavily on standardized tests and "fitness" reports prepared by superior officers to decide who will be promoted and who will be allowed to remain on active duty.

It also enforces strict standards for weight and physical fitness for its members. They are scaled by age and sex. In the Army, a

20-year-old male must be able to do 42 push-ups, 52 sit-ups, and run two miles in under 16 minutes. A female the same age must do 18 push-ups, 50 sit-ups, and run two miles in under 19 minutes. A 30-year-old male is given little slack; 38 push-ups, 42 sit-ups, and two miles within 18 minutes are required.

Some argue that the improved pay and benefits GI's receive today entitles the command to demand more from its troops than it did in the past. A private first class (PFC) today earns about $800 a month, compared with $100-plus in the Vietnam War years. Most of the old ramshackle wooden barracks in which enlisted GI's used to live have been pulled down and replaced with air-conditioned brick apartment units. Those who live off base often receive tax-free subsidies of several hundred dollars each month to help with rent or mortgage payments.

Each of the services administers some form of written proficiency tests to most enlisted personnel each year. In the Army, an exam called the Skills Qualification Test (SQT) is given annually for each military occupational specialty. These test scores are used in determining promotions and even retention in the service.

In addition to these physical and job-proficiency tests, the military also regularly tests *everyone* on active duty for drug use and for exposure to the HIV virus, which is believed to cause AIDS. Urine samples are collected to test for marijuana, cocaine, and other drug residues. Blood testing is used to detect HIV antibodies. (See Chapter 5 for more details about these two test programs).

JOB HAZARDS

You should be aware that service in the peacetime military can be hazardous to your health. Over 10,000 GI's have been killed accidentally during training or combat exercises from 1979 to 1987. The actual facts surrounding many of these accidents are often not disclosed even to the next of kin because of military secrecy rules. Although internal reports may provide information about what caused a particular accident, these are not generally released to the public or even shared with GI's who may be at risk.

For example, repeated accidents with the M151 truck killed over 80 GI's before roll bars and shoulder harnesses were finally

installed. A classified report about one of these deaths commented, "It's an old story. The details vary, but it's always the same
vehicle [M151] . . . the thing likes to roll over."

Often, these reports blame individual GI's for accidents rather
than looking for deeper causes, such as design defects. For instance, an Orange County, CA, newspaper disclosed in December
1988 that military reports often attributed helicopter crashes to
"pilot error." In sixty-two different crashes studied by the newspaper (in which 132 GI's died), it found that the pilots were wearing night-vision goggles. Goggle manufacturers were quoted as
saying that these goggles were not intended for use at the speed
helicopters fly and that such use would impair vision.

Air crashes of both cargo jets and helicopters continue to
claim victims. Between October 1988 and March 1989, two Air
Force cargo jets crashed, killing a total of twenty-five GI's. In
just one month, March 1989, three separate helicopter crashes,
two in South Korea and one in Arizona, killed forty-two more
soldiers.

Some critics have charged that the Pentagon is slow to correct
dangerous practices because the Supreme Court ruled years ago
that the military cannot be sued for injuries to GI's, no matter
how negligent its commanders may have been. This special immunity is discussed later, in the section on military medical care.

The Supreme Court also closed another possible avenue of redress for families of victims when it ruled in June 1988 that cor-
porations that manufacture equipment for the Pentagon *cannot*
be sued for injuries caused by their product, provided they manufactured it to government specifications and known defects
were disclosed to the government.

MILITARY LIFE

When you join the military, you enter a society largely separate
from civilian life. Most career military people spend their active-
duty years on vast military bases that are self-contained, small
cities. Everything from the shopping malls to the sewers and
power lines are provided by the military. Most children of GI's
stationed in the United States attend civilian public schools, although the Pentagon still operates a number of school systems,
called "Section Six" schools. Plans are underway to turn these
over to civilian school boards wherever possible.

Regular moves from one base to another, sometimes thousands of miles apart, are a fact of life for nearly all military families. A survey of Army families conducted in 1988 found that 81 percent of all families had moved at least once within the past three years; 23 percent had moved three or more times during the same period.

Rank is very important to military people. It's the first thing that is usually noticed about a person. There is really nothing in civilian society like the military concept of rank. One reason rank is so important is that it is one of the few things that distinguishes someone from everyone else. Remember, service members live in look-alike housing, wear the same uniforms, and don't usually make enough money to show off with cars, jewelry, or furs. In fact, spouses and children of GI's are sometimes identified by reference to their sponsor's rank.

The following brief description of each service branch may help you to understand what life in the military is like.

Army Life

The oldest and largest service branch, the Army currently has about 744,000 people on active duty, with about one third of them stationed outside the United States at any given time. This branch is slated to undergo further reductions over the next four years, bringing it down to about 630,000 people by 1995. As one of the largest employers in America, the Army offers a vast array of jobs, from dog handler to pharmacy technician.

The general "tone" of each of the service branches is set by its primary combat mission. The Army's job is to conduct ground combat operations using a combination of infantry, artillery, and armored units, supported by helicopters. About one in four soldiers is actually a member of a fighting unit, with the bulk of Army personnel providing everything from bookkeeping to ammunition supply.

For example, Fort Bragg, NC, is home to the Army's 82d Airborne Division. Although only a portion of the 41,000 GI's at Bragg actually parachute out of airplanes, the airborne mission influences everyone on post, even those who work as clerks or welders.

People get the impression (which recruiters sometimes encourage) that a support job like finance or nursing is pretty much like a nine-to-five job on the "outside." This can be misleading. Everyone on active duty is technically "on call" twenty-four hours a day and is subject to the military's strict criminal code during most of that time.

Inspections and formations, at which attendance is mandatory, can occur regularly in the Army, no matter what one's rank or job. Extra duty, such as working overtime or on weekends without additional pay, is also common.

Many Army commanders today take a personal interest in encouraging the physical fitness of their troops. Even soldiers who work in noncombat jobs like public affairs or supply are often ordered to spend several mornings a week on calisthenics training *before* reporting for work.

If you are assigned to a combat-arms branch, you can expect to be sent for field training in remote parts of the United States and abroad. For instance, about 80,000 infantry troops who work with armored or mechanized units are sent annually to the National Training Center in California's Mojave desert. "Light" infantry, Airborne, and Ranger units are sent for special training at Fort Chafee's Joint Readiness Training Center in rural Arkansas.

Both of these bases are located in isolated areas with harsh terrain. Everyone wears MILES gear (Multiple Integrated Laser Engagement System) so that "kills" and "wounds" are electronically recorded. Visiting units are put through realistic combat exercises in which they "fight" other troops who use Soviet equipment and Soviet-style military tactics. As a rule, the "Soviets" win the battles, partly because they are used to working together and know the terrain. Some GI's report that they were challenged by the actual exercises, but disliked the long stretches of inactivity.

Tens of thousands of soliders are also sent to West Germany and Korea each year to participate in "war games" with troops from those countries. The largest such exercise is "Reforger" (Return of Forces to Germany), which has been held almost every year since 1983. About 125,000 soldiers from the American, Canadian, and West German armies spend about six to eight weeks on bivouac, often in the snow and rain, conducting simulated combat against make-believe aggressors from the Warsaw Pact armies.

The annual "Team Spirit" exercise in Korea involves 60,000 U.S. troops (mostly Army), of which at least one third are brought over from the United States to practice with 140,000 South Korean troops. The Pentagon states that this exercise, which began in 1975, "demonstrates [our] resolve to deter aggression in the Korean peninsula and increases readiness."

These complicated war games can be dangerous. During the 1989 event, a helicopter carrying thirty-seven Marines crashed in an isolated mountain region, killing twenty-two and injuring the rest. A few days earlier, another helicopter crashed, killing the four Marines on board.

The military calls its annual "Brim Frost" exercise, which takes place each winter in Alaska, the "premier cold-weather training in the free world." During the 1989 exercise, which was conducted during a blizzard with temperatures dropping to 60° below zero, 26,000 Army, Air Force, and Marine troops practiced maneuvers. Tragedy struck again when eight Canadian soldiers were killed in a cargo plane crash at the site.

These exercises are designed to be as realistic as possible, so troops are kept continually on alert, with the training day lasting up to twenty hours, seven days a week.

About ten years ago, the Army began experimenting with "light" infantry divisions that can be sent, on short notice, to fight in "trouble spots" anywhere in the world. It has created five new "light" divisions, with about 10,500 GI's in each, which are designed for rapid deployment ("wheels up" in eighteen hours) via C-141 cargo jets.

Lacking the usual tank and artillery support, these units are trained to engage in highly mobile, small-unit tactics. They regularly practice night fighting and train in extreme climates like tropical jungles and Arctic mountains. Critics have questioned how a division short on vehicles and firepower would fare against a well-armed foe. In fact, these units have few tanks, nor do they have an effective and portable antitank weapon.

Each brigade within a division rotates being "on call" for two weeks at a time. During this period, GI's must stay close enough to the base so that they can report, in battle gear, within two hours. In the 82d Airborne, units spend six weeks on what is called "division ready force" (DRF) status. If you leave the post, you have to phone in every hour or so to make sure that a "call-out" order hasn't been issued. As one former Airborne Ranger Dave Allen put it, "These 'call outs' and 'alerts' get old real fast."

The five "light" divisions are stationed at five Army bases: Fort Ord, CA; Fort Richardson, AL; Fort Drum, NY; Schofield Barracks, HI; and Fort Belvoir, VA, which is a National Guard unit.

The Army's Problems Today

The disaster of the Vietnam War hit the Army the hardest of any of the service branches. A number of books written by military officers and scholars have concluded that some of the problems identified during Vietnam have continued to plague the military. As evidence of this, they point to such failures as the bungled attempt to rescue the Iranian embassy hostages in 1980, and the Beirut occupation, during which 241 Marines were needlessly killed in 1983.

These writers trace some of the Army's current problems to a command structure that has grown increasingly top-heavy and bureaucratic. Many believe that the poor quality of combat leadership in Vietnam was caused by a "ticket-punching" system whereby officers rotated in and out on six-month tours. They stayed just long enough to acquire career "brownie points," but not long enough to develop leadership skills. Enlisted personnel were limited to a one-year tour, to appease public opinion about the war. This interfered with the development of unit loyalty, which boosts morale and motivation. One observer noted the negative impact of this "revolving door" policy, "We weren't in Vietnam thirteen years, but only for a year thirteen times."

These critics have identified a number of problem areas for the Army (and the other branches) that are summarized below.

- *A promotion system that rewards conformity.* Officers who accumulate graduate degrees or who can employ corporate management techniques are promoted, often without regard to their leadership abilities.

- *A command structure that has grown too large and top-heavy.* In 1983, the ratio of mid-level officers to enlisted personnel was *four times* higher than it was during World War II. Too many layers of bureaucracy stifle individual initiative and make it difficult for military units to respond to crises.

- *Failure to develop reliable, yet simple weapons.* The Sergeant York Air Defense gun and the Sheridan tank are two "lemons" on which the Army has wasted billions. Analyst Edward Luttwak sums up the cause: "Over-elaborate organizations show the same preference for over-elaborate weapons."

- *Misuse of officer evaluation reports.* Grade inflation and mutual backscratching have produced a "zero defect" system that requires a near-perfect score for promotion. Also, the fact that a soldier's evaluations are prepared by his immediate supervisors increases the pressure to conform and not ask questions.

- *Over-reliance on statistics.* In Vietnam, the Army measured its progress by counting Vietnamese bodies. The higher the "body count," they thought, the closer we were to victory.

- *Tolerance by the command of illegal violence (war crimes).* "Grunts" in Vietnam implemented military policies such as "free-fire zones," which led to atrocities. However, when the press learned about wholesale shooting of civilians, such as the My Lai massacre, in which over 300 Vietnamese died, only a few low-ranking officers and NCO's were ever court-martialed. No one in a position of high authority who planned the overall operations was ever held responsible.

Successful militaries have traditionally been led by strong men and women who weren't afraid to make bold and decisive moves during battle. Many critics feel that most Army officers today have become bland "yes-men." A successful tactician like General George Patton, whose individual style offended some of his peers during World War II, probably wouldn't prosper in today's Army.

Navy Life

The Reagan Administration came into office promising to increase defense spending and expand U.S. military power. The White House prepared a secret blueprint, called the "Defense Guidelines," that ordered the Pentagon to adopt a more aggressive military posture throughout the world. Later, some military officers complained that their units were being asked to do too much, given their resources.

The Navy, which was the largest beneficiary of the military build-up during the Reagan years, embarked on a major shipbuilding campaign. Although President Reagan's dream of a 600-ship Navy was never realized, the fleet was substantially enlarged and sent to world "trouble spots" such as the Persian Gulf more frequently and for longer periods of time. This, of course, increased the workload on Navy personnel.

At any given time today, roughly 250,000 sailors (out of 580,000 total) are assigned to sea duty. The ratio of "ship" to "shore" duty varies, depending on a sailor's rating (job), but it's common to be assigned 44 to 48 months of sea duty, before 24 months of shore assignment. During a 20-year career, a sailor will typically spend 14 years on "sea duty" status. During these periods, a sailor can expect to be gone from home for a 5- or 6-month cruise to the Mediterranean or Pacific regions about once a year.

Serving aboard one of the Navy's 14 aircraft carriers is like working in a densely populated small town. The largest carrier, the nuclear-powered USS Nimitz, carries a crew of 6,300. Most of the other carriers have crews of from 5,000 to 5,500 people. The flight deck of the Nimitz is 4½ acres and can accommodate 95 jet fighters. Each carrier leads a battlegroup, consisting of at least 9 warships, as well as other support ships. Three of these carriers, which date back to World War II, may need to be removed from service soon. If budget problems prevent their replacement (which seems likely), this will add to the workload and sea time of the remaining carriers.

Sailors who have served aboard carriers report that when flight operations are underway, the noise of jets taking off and landing, and the sound of the launch catapult can be heard throughout the ship.

At sea, most sailors work long hours and live in less-than-ideal conditions. It is common for sailors to be assigned "port and starboard watches," during which they are on duty twelve hours, followed by twelve hours off. Often, sailors must stand watch and perform other duties in *addition* to doing their assigned job. "General quarters" drills, when everyone rushes to preassigned battle stations, are sometimes called every day. If this wakes you from a much-needed sleep, too bad! Also, many enlisted people must clean their berthing and mess areas in preparation for daily inspections by the ship's officers.

Living conditions aboard ship range from barely adequate to primitive. Thirty to forty sailors may be assigned to a single berthing area with triple-deck bunks stacked so close together that one can barely turn over in bed. Each sailor has a small trunk that hangs below his bed in which to store his clothes and personal items. On the other hand, officers live in staterooms that they might share with another officer, depending on their rank.

Aboard some ships, living space is so limited that there are not enough beds to go around. In this case, a peculiar Navy custom called "hot racking" is practiced. Sailors share the use of the bed, switching on and off with each other as one goes on duty and another comes off!

Some ships restrict the amount of water that sailors can use to shower. On these ships, sailors are allowed just enough water to lather up. Then they're given just a shot of water for rinsing. Anyone who uses too much water is subject to punishment. When sailors are allowed to take a normal shower, they call it a "Hollywood."

During a six-month cruise, sailors may receive no more than ten days of liberty in foreign ports. While in "liberty port," many sailors still will be required to perform their shipboard assignments. They can go ashore only when their work is finished and usually receive only "Cinderella" liberty, meaning that they must be back on ship by midnight. Officers, by contrast, can stay ashore all night.

Some shipboard jobs can be dangerous, such as gunner's mate. Gunner's mates fire the huge 16- and 8-inch guns aboard destroyers and heavy cruisers. In April 1989, 47 sailors were killed when 550 pounds of gunpowder exploded inside a gun turret on the USS *Iowa*. It set off secondary explosions and fires that burned for over an hour in the gun turret. One former *Iowa* sailor, Bill Humienny, told reporters that the turret was "like a tomb" when it was sealed during firing. Everyone on the upper levels was killed; a few in the bottom chamber survived.

The USS *Iowa* is one of four huge World War II battleships that the Reagan Administration refurbished and restored to use. The huge guns on these ships use a firing system that was developed half a century ago. Bags of highly explosive gunpowder are inserted directly into the firing chamber. Some have speculated that vintage World War II gunpowder or shells may have somehow caused the explosion. Others have argued that it was caused by the "HERO Effect" (Hazard of Electromagnetic Radiation to Ordnance). Ammunition can be touched off if it is exposed to one of several sources of electromagnetic radiation, such as lightning, radio, television, or radar transmissions, or other electrostatic discharges.

After an extensive investigation, the Navy released a report in September 1989 that satisfied few observers. It attributed the disaster to a "wrongful intentional act . . . most probably committed" by a gunner's mate who, the investigators concluded, was suicidal because another sailor had rejected his homosexual overtures.

In hearings held by the House and Senate Armed Services committees, witnesses criticized many aspects of the Navy's investigation. In March 1990, the House committee issued a report that rejected the Navy's conclusion that a single suicidal sailor had caused the explosion. As ABC's Pentagon correspondent observed, "this . . . spares the Navy the anguish of contemplating whether its own malfeasance is due all or part of the blame." A similar explosion in a gun turret killed twenty sailors and injured thirty-six others aboard the heavy cruiser *Newport News* off the coast of Vietnam in 1972.

Other seagoing jobs, like engineman and boiler technician, are physically very taxing and can be dangerous as well. In May 1989, a fire broke out in the engine room of the USS *White Plains* that killed six and injured five others. These people, who are called "snipes" in Navy lingo, work deep in the bowels of a ship, where temperatures routinely exceed 100°. They must sometimes come topside for short periods to recover from the extreme water and salt loss they suffer in the hold.

Navy veterans tell me that new arrivals at any ship can expect to spend their first three months aboard as messcooks or doing other menial tasks. These cooks begin work at dawn, performing the worst kitchen jobs until well into the evening. Some work as waiters in the officers' dining rooms.

Remember, when you are aboard ship (or assigned to one in port), the ancient Navy tradition of "drumhead justice" is still in effect. This means that if you're charged with a minor offense at a "Captain's Mast," you are automatically guilty under Article 15 of the Uniform Code of Military Justice. You cannot try to prove your innocence at a trial. The only thing that can be appealed to higher authority is the terms of punishment (see Chapter 5 for a full discussion).

Duty aboard one of the Navy's 140 nuclear or conventionally powered submarines can also be quite arduous. These subs, each of which carry about 150 crewmembers, are usually armed with numerous nuclear warheads. An old joke has it that nuclear subs only come to the surface once every four years—so that the crew can reenlist! This *is* an exaggeration, but subs commonly go on patrols during which they're submerged for up to seventy days at a stretch. Within the Navy, submariners are considered an elite group in terms of their intelligence and skills.

The Navy has two types of submarines: attack subs and ballistic missile subs, which are called "boomers." The 102 attack submarines are used to hunt down and pursue Soviet and other "unfriendly" subs. In wartime, they would seek to destroy them. "Boomers" by comparison, operate at low speeds and maintain constant radio contact with the command. The 37 ballistic subs practice for one primary job—to launch their deadly missiles at Soviet targets from predetermined positions. Among submariners, service aboard attack subs is considered more exciting and challenging than service on missile boats.

Two environmental groups published a report in June 1989 that found that over 2,000 major accidents have occurred among nuclear navies in the period since World War II. The study, which is titled "Naval Accidents 1945–88" used declassified Navy reports. In addition to providing details about the various accidents, which claimed about 2,800 lives, it also pinpointed the location of 50 nuclear warheads and 9 nuclear reactors that have settled on the ocean floor.

The study also provides the first public accounts of three nuclear accidents involving U.S. ships that had been kept secret. In one, a hydrogen bomb was lost when a Skyhawk jet rolled off the aircraft carrier USS *Ticonderoga* eighty miles from Japan in 1965. The second involved a serious nuclear propulsion accident aboard the USS *Guardfish* in 1973, after which five sailors were hospitalized for radiation monitoring. In the third, a fire aboard the USS *Belknap* in 1975 nearly engulfed the ship's nuclear weapons while it was sailing off the coast of Italy. Coauthor William Arkin told reporters that while naval accidents can never be eliminated, those that involve nuclear weapons or reactors are the most dangerous.

A Navy survey conducted in 1988 found that separation from family, frequent transfers, and low pay were the three principal reasons sailors gave for quitting the service.

The Navy and Marine Corps still observe the tradition of a weekly "field day." This means all hands are required to spend several hours cleaning up their barracks or work areas. In the Marines, this event usually takes place on Thursday night.

Over a 200-year period, the Navy has developed many customs. Some people consider the Navy to be the most tradition-oriented branch. Also, the line between officer and enlisted personnel is probably the sharpest in the Navy.

Air Force Life

This is the newest branch of the armed forces, created as a separate service in 1947. Because the Air Force's primary mission is to bomb and fight from the air and to launch guided missiles, it emphasizes technology and scientific knowledge.

Air Force personnel often have an elitist attitude toward the other branches. Its members tend to look down upon (no pun intended) their military brothers who slog along on the ground carrying puny rifles and backpacks.

In the Air Force, officers who fly planes do the actual fighting, while enlisted personnel serve in the rear—the opposite of the other services. Since the great majority of Air Force jobs are non-combatant, this branch has the highest proportion of females.

Pilots traditionally have dominated the Air Force hierarchy and have been able to stop any shift away from piloted aircraft. Some analysts are critical of this "Top Gun syndrome," arguing that unmanned aircraft would be less expensive and could be more effective in many situations.

Life on an Air Force base is less strict and regimented than it is in the other branches. Inspections occur infrequently, with some bases using maids to take care of the barracks. According to Hal Harris, a recently retired officer, most Air Force people (except flight crews) regard their assignment as "just a job." Many enlisted people also have part-time civilian jobs as a way of making ends meet. Harris commented that Air Force discipline has become much more "lax" than when he joined in the early sixties.

The Air Force operates many air bases throughout the United States and abroad. A large percentage of their domestic bases are located in the South, Southwest, and California.

Marine Life

The members of this branch are known throughout the military for their intense pride and competitiveness. Without much encouragement, a Marine will tell you that the Corps is superior, especially to the Army. The Corps' primary mission is to conduct amphibious combat assaults using lightly armed troops, who are trained to fight at some distance from their support elements.

The phrase, "every Marine a rifleman" is taken seriously throughout the Corps. Marine Commandant Al Grey sums it up: "The only reason the United States needs a Marine Corps is to fight and win wars. Our leadership training is dedicated [to] preparing commanders to lead our Marines in combat."

During a visit to the Marines training base at Parris Island, SC, I watched as males and females rappelled with ropes from a fifty-foot tower at the crack of dawn. One by one, the Marines stepped to the edge of the tower, shouted "Marine Corps!" and leaped, using a handbrake on the rappelling rope to stop their fall just as they hit the ground. They turned out to be *cooks* who had volunteered for this exercise because they wanted to get in some extra practice! If you don't enjoy a very physical, bare-knuckle style of life, the Marine Corps is not the place for you.

Most Marines serving in the United States are stationed at Camp LeJeune in North Carolina or Camp Pendleton near San Diego. Another division is stationed in Japan with part of another deployed in Hawaii. Marines also serve in small detachments aboard Navy ships and guarding Naval bases, particularly in the Orient. Another 1,400 specially trained Marines serve as guards at U.S. embassies and consulates throughout the world.

Some military analysts argue that the idea of Marines storming beachheads during amphibious assaults is outdated. They suggest that ordinary troops deployed by helicopters would make more sense. Just don't try telling *that* to a Marine!

Coast Guard Life

The Coast Guard's primary mission is to conduct search and rescue missions and to enforce U.S. and state laws in international waters along America's borders. Most Coast Guard people are assigned to relatively small ships that perform a wide variety of difficult jobs, from boarding boats suspected of smuggling drugs or illegal immigrants to aiding boats in distress. One Coast Guard veteran estimated that 90 percent of his training was devoted to law enforcement and boat handling.

Typically, a Coast Guard station is quite small, with perhaps thirty crew members. The small size often creates a strong camaraderie. It also can magnify personality differences in an unpleasant way.

Coast Guard stations are mostly located along the Atlantic and Pacific coastlines in resort areas where the cost of living is quite high. Because many of the smaller stations provide only limited housing, living "on the economy" (as military people call living off post) can eat up all of your pay.

The Coast Guard uses boats that vary in size from a 378-foot craft with over 100 crew members to a 95-foot patrol boat with only 12 crew members. The larger boats can patrol at sea for a month before returning to port. The small boats usually go out and return the same day.

The dramatic increase in drug smuggling from Latin America and the Caribbean has made Coast Guard duty much more dangerous and stressful than it was in the past. Petty Officer John Childs, of Marathon, FL, has served fourteen years as a "coastie." "I joined to do 'search and rescue' and to fix boat engines. During my first six years, I never saw a weapon except on the target range," John recalls. "Now, we never get under way (go to sea) without a flak jacket, pistol, can of Mace, expandable nightstick, shotgun, and an M-16."

Childs believes that tougher drug laws that impose long prison terms have made smugglers more ruthless. He cited a recent case in his area of Florida where a boat suspected of drug smuggling collided with a small pleasure craft and then left two people to drown rather than stop to lend assistance. Everyone who goes out on Coast Guard patrols today must qualify on the target range with the .45-caliber pistol, riot shotgun, and M-16.

The constant patrolling can also be hard on a service member's family. "This isn't the service to be in if you're looking for a stable home life," John Childs comments. "I've seen the Coast Guard tear up a lot of marriages because of the time at sea, the transfers, and so on."

Because of the drug epidemic and the huge increase in pleasure boats (from 9 million in 1970 to 15 million in 1987), many Coast Guard people put in far more than 40 hours a week. At many stations, everyone must stand a 24-hour watch every three or four days. This duty is in addition to one's regular job. Childs, a diesel mechanic, estimates that he has worked a *minimum* of ninety hours a week in recent years!

The Coast Guard also operates a network of LORAN (long-range navigation) stations that are scattered around the world. These facilities transmit radio signals that serve as navigational aids, mainly for ships. Some of these stations, which typically have 20 to 30 crew members, are located on tiny islands hundreds of miles out to sea. LORAN personnel are supplied mostly by cargo planes that visit periodically. This duty, which normally consists of one-year hitches, is recommended only for those who crave true peace and quiet. In recent years, the Navy's warships have relied increasingly on the new NAVSTAR satellites. Their signal is less susceptible to jamming than is the LORAN system, should a shooting war break out.

REPORTING FRAUD, MISMANAGEMENT, OR WASTE

The Department of Defense has established a toll-free number (800-424-9098) to encourage GI's to report instances of fraud, mismanagement, or other abuses. In recent years, the service has averaged about 1,000 calls a month. According to the Pentagon, about 10 percent of these calls result in investigations.

A press handout for the program promises that "all calls are confidential." GI's who call the "hotline" are encouraged to identify themselves, although allegations by anonymous "whistleblowers" will be investigated. Congress recently beefed up laws protecting those who report wrongdoing. The military's Inspector General is now required to "expeditiously investigate" whistleblowers' allegations of retaliation. One reason to identify yourself is the cash reward (up to $10,000) that is sometimes paid if your report saves the military money.

Despite these laws, I believe that GI's face a risk of being a target for harassment when they identify themselves. You should carefully weigh the pros and cons. Remember, superior officers in the military have several ways to retaliate against a lower-ranking person.

COMPENSATION

The old stereotype of the impoverished soldier who escapes his dreary barracks on Saturday night by hitching a ride to a base-town honky-tonk no longer has much validity. In 1963, for instance, a recruit's pay was $40 a month. In 1989, the average enlisted person's annual gross pay (including housing allowances) was $21,108, while the average officer grossed $43,164.

The military offers various types of compensation other than basic pay, including 33 special or incentive compensation plans for hazardous or extra stressful duty. For example, recruiters, drill instructors, and career counselors receive "special duty" pay (up to $270 a month) because their jobs require many extra hours of work. A partial listing of compensation plans follows.

Basic Pay

A service member's gross pay is calculated by his rank and his years in service. With few exceptions, everyone with the same rank and time served will receive identical pay, regardless of performance records. A recruit just out of boot camp in 1989 earned $646 a month, while a sergeant with four years in that rank received $1,041. A major with three years in that rank got $2,472 a month. This pay is subject to both federal income tax and Social Security. Most states arrange to have income taxes withheld from the pay of GI's who claim legal residency. In the last few years, military pay has been increased approximately 4 percent annually.

Enlisted people who live on post are provided with three meals a day in the mess hall. In recent years, many mess halls have begun providing some alternatives to the traditionally high calorie (and high cholesterol) military diet. Some have installed salad bars and "light" menu items like fish and steamed vegetables to compete with salisbury steak with mashed potatoes and gravy. If a GI cannot eat in the mess hall because of his duty, he will be paid a Basic Allowance for Subsistence (BAS), which can range from $5.27 to $8.53 per day, depending on his rank. Anyone who has permission to live off post, either single or married, will usually receive BAS. All officers are paid BAS, which amounted to $119.61 a month in 1989.

Enlistment and Reenlistment Bonuses

The military has found it necessary to pay cash bonuses to recruit and retain people who perform certain jobs. These fall into two categories; "3-D" combat-arms jobs ("dirty, difficult, and dangerous"), and highly skilled jobs in the medical, aviation, and nuclear fields. The military has suffered a steady "brain drain" in these jobs because civilian employers offer better pay and working conditions.

Combat-arms bonuses range from $2,000 to $8,000 for a three-year commitment. Most of these are paid to reenlistees, not recruits. Bonuses for critical skills can go as high as $40,000, although most are in the $10,000 to $15,000 range. Pilots currently receive up to $12,000 in annual bonuses, while medical doctors in specialties like surgery and orthopedics sometimes are paid as much as $40,000 for multi-year reenlistments.

Jobs that qualify for bonuses change periodically, depending on manpower needs. Your recruiter will be eager to tell you about any bonuses for which you may qualify.

Hostile Fire Pay

This is the peacetime equivalent of "combat pay" that GI's have received in past wars. Anyone who is assigned to an area that is designated as a "hostile fire zone" receives an extra (taxable) payment of $110 a month. Anyone who serves in the zone qualifies, whether on land, aboard ship, or in the air; he doesn't have to be in danger of harm. Sailors and Marines serving aboard Navy ships in the Persian Gulf began receiving this pay in August 1987. After Iran and Iraq declared a cease-fire in late 1988, U.S. officials rescinded the "hostile zone" designation.

Sea Pay and Submarine Duty Pay

As mentioned earlier, duty aboard ship or sub is no picnic. In recognition of this, sailors (E/4 and above) are paid an extra $50 to $520 for each month they are at sea. Marines, Coast Guard, and even members of the Army also qualify for this pay while they are aboard ship.

Submariners receive special pay of $75 to $355, depending on their rank, for each month they are "under way." Missile-carrying subs on which two crews rotate, give all crew members this pay even when they are not at sea.

Hazardous Duty Pay

There are ten jobs for which the military currently provides hazardous pay. These include parachuting, demolitions with explosives, flight deck crews on aircraft carriers, and handlers of toxic fuels and pesticides. In a break with tradition, no distinction is made between enlisted and officers; they both receive the same stipend of $120 each month. Deep-sea divers qualify for a special pay of $100 to $300 per month, depending on their level of skill.

Flight Pay

Pilots, navigators, weapons officers, and flight surgeons are eligible for flight pay under several categories, ranging from $125 to $400 per month. After twelve years or so, officers on flight status automatically receive this pay whether or not they go up in planes.

Enlisted flight crew members qualify under a different program that pays from $110 to $200 a month. Unlike officers, however, they must actually fly in order to qualify.

Foreign Duty Pay

Most GI's who are assigned outside the United States will receive this token payment, which ranges from $8 to $22.50 per month.

Cost of Living Allowance (Overseas)

This allowance is paid to many GI's stationed abroad to help them survive the high prices and unfavorable exchange rates for dollars that they often encounter in Western Europe and Japan. These payments are based on a complicated formula that takes into account the country, number of dependents, and rank of the GI.

Overseas Incentive Pay

To reduce the high cost of replacing overseas personnel, the military encourages GI's serving abroad to extend their tours. As a reward for a one-year extension, an enlisted GI can choose one of the following: $80 extra pay each month, thirty extra days of leave, or fifteen extra days of leave with a free round-trip air ticket to the United States.

PENSION

Most military people consider this to be their single best personnel benefit. Once a GI has served a minimum of twenty years, he is eligible to "retire" and immediately begin receiving a military pension for the rest of his life. The pension payment, which is taxable, is calculated by a complicated formula that has been adjusted recently to reduce pension payments. GI's who entered the military before September 1980 will still receive a pension based on 50 percent of their final month's pay (75 percent for those with 30 years). However, newer members will have their pension calculated on an average of their highest thirty-six months of pay. The net effect of this is that they will receive between 10 to 12½ percent less than older veterans.

Pensions as Marital Property

About ten years ago, Congress adopted the Former Spouses Protection Act. Essentially, this allows the state courts handling divorces to award up to half of a military pension to a former spouse for alimony, child support, or property distribution. Any marriage that lasted at least ten years of a GI's active-duty period is covered by this law.

Former spouses who don't remarry are also allowed, under certain conditions, to enjoy free military medical care and commissary privileges.

HOUSING ALLOWANCES

There are basically two programs to assist GI's with off-base housing costs. Basic Allowance for Quarters (BAQ), and Variable Housing Allowance (VHA) or Overseas Housing Allowance (OHA).

In general, unmarried enlisted personnel (E/6 and below) will be assigned to live in a barracks on post if space is available. If a GI chooses to live off base anyway, he'll have to absorb all the costs of living off post, except for a token BAQ ($7.20 to $17.70 monthly).

Enlisted personnel who are married (65 percent of the force today) as well as officers and senior NCO's (E/7 and above) will receive housing subsidies if they choose to live off base.

With real estate prices escalating rapidly throughout much of the United States, many enlisted families would prefer to live in rent-free military housing on base. Unfortunately, many military bases today have shortages of such housing, and waits of a year or more are common. For instance, an Army survey of the Fort

Bragg, NC, area in 1988 found a deficit of 4,160 units of "affordable" housing for lower-ranking enlisted personnel.

Every base has a housing office that manages military-owned apartments and assists GI's with off-base rentals. By law, GI's are forbidden to rent or buy from anyone who practices discrimination based on race, sex, religion, national origin, or disability.

Basic Allowance for Quarters (BAQ)

This payment is computed with a complicated formula that is supposed to subsidize about 61 percent of civilian housing costs. An E/4 with dependents would receive a nontaxable monthly BAQ of $303, while a major with dependents would get $577.

In 1988, the Pentagon estimated the median *actual* housing cost for these two ranks at $497 and $946, respectively. One could reasonably ask why the military's estimate of housing costs differs because of rank. Presumably, a family of four needs more or less the same space, whether mom or dad is a sergeant or a colonel. The answer, of course, is "RHIP" (Rank Has Its Privileges)!

Variable Housing Allowance (VHA)

This program was created by Congress about ten years ago to help GI's cope with escalating housing costs. These payments are calculated so that when they're combined with BAQ, they should provide a GI with about 79 percent of his civilian housing cost. Differing VHA ranges are set for 350 areas of the United States. In some areas (mostly rural, where housing is cheap), no VHA is paid.

Military personnel assigned to urban areas on the east and west coasts often complain that the cost estimates on which BAQ and VHA payments are based are unreasonably low. They have to make up the difference out of their regular pay.

Overseas Housing Allowances (OHA)

Many U.S. bases abroad also suffer housing shortages. GI's stationed abroad receive BAQ payments on the same basis as in the United States. Like VHA, OHA was created to help service members cope with high housing costs, particularly in Western Europe. There are 1,500 different OHA rates based on locale. Combined with BAQ, this is intended to pay about 80 percent of actual costs. These payments are generally higher than VHA in the States.

A married GI who is serving an unaccompanied tour (without dependents) may be entitled to Family Separation Allowance if no government quarters are available. This amounts to the no-dependents BAQ rate.

Travel and Per Diem

Any time a GI is ordered to make a "permanent change of station," he will receive flat rate payments to move. If he uses his own car, he will be paid $50 per day for himself, and an additional $37.50 per day each for his spouse and any dependents over 12 years old. Dependents under twelve qualify for $25 a day. These payments are based on the assumption that the family will travel at least 350 miles a day.

When a GI is transferred to a new duty station overseas, the military will pay all travel costs for him and his family, provided that the command has given permission for an "accompanied tour." If it hasn't, then the GI will have to pay all family travel costs out of his own pocket.

A service member also will receive per diem pay for hotel and food costs while he is traveling on military business. This payment will vary depending on a complicated formula. In New York City, for example, a GI will receive the highest per diem paid by the military of $147 per day.

Shipment of Household Goods

Each time a GI makes a permanent change of station (usually at least once every three years), he is entitled to have his possessions and furniture shipped free of charge. Weight allowances are based on rank, with an E/4 with dependents permitted 8,000 pounds. A major with dependents is allowed up to 17,000 pounds.

The military will also ship one private automobile for each GI assigned overseas. Strict pollution controls and the high cost of gasoline and repairs deter some GI's from using this benefit.

The Pentagon also allows minor GI dependents who attend college in the United States one free trip each year on a "space-available" basis. However, since many dependents are competing for scarce plane seats during the same holiday periods, many military families find that they must purchase commercial air tickets for their children.

Vacations (Annual Leave)

The military is perfectly democratic in at least one respect; everyone, regardless of rank, receives the same thirty vacation days each year. Since you can only be paid for sixty accumulated (unused) leave days when you leave the military, you should use your leave days regularly. If you are on sick leave or ordered to take special "rest and rehabilitation" leave, this will not be counted against your thirty days.

Clothing Allowance

Each service branch makes a lump-sum payment annually to help GI's maintain their uniforms. The Army currently pays male GI's $194.40 and females $216.00 a year for this purpose.

PROMOTION OF ENLISTED PERSONNEL

There is only one promotion in the military that is automatic—from E/1 to E/2. Every GI will receive this stripe after six months service, assuming that no bar to promotion has been imposed for misconduct. GI's who have helped recruiters sign up other recruits may receive accelerated promotion to E/2 when they finish boot camp. Also, unit commanders may reward outstanding performers with early promotion. Every enlisted person is assigned a pay grade, ranging from E/1 through E/9. Officers' pay grades go from O-1 through O-10.

After one year, E/2's are eligible for promotion to the next grade, provided that their unit commander recommends it. Again, early promotion can be used to recognize exemplary GI's.

After E/3, all further promotions depend on the vacancies available in each rank. Usually, one must serve at least two years before being promoted to E/4. This is the rank of "corporal" in the Army and Marines. The Air Force calls it "senior airman" and the Navy "petty officer 3rd class."

In the Army, candidates for E/4 will sometimes be required to take the Skills Qualification Test (SQT) in their job specialty and to appear before a local selection board.

The distinction between the lower enlisted ranks and noncommissioned officers (NCO's) is an important one in the military. For this reason, promotion to NCO status (E/5 and above) is a much more involved process than it is for the lower ranks. Each service has its own rules and procedures that are too complicated to describe in other than general terms.

Essentially, candidates for these ranks compete on a servicewide basis. Local unit commanders have less authority over promotion decisions at this level, although their input is still important.

In the Army, each candidate's record is reviewed by a promotion board consisting of the senior NCO's and the commander of his unit. Each candidate will receive at least one Enlisted Evaluation Report (EER) or a Noncommissioned Officer Evaluation Report each year. This evaluation is prepared by his immediate supervisor and must be endorsed by another officer.

The evaluator and endorser both rate a candidate on such things as physical fitness, ability to communicate, military skills, and appearance and leadership potential.

If a soldier receives an evaluation that he believes erroneous or grossly unjust, he can appeal it to higher authority. Generally, he needs to collect statements of rebuttal by others who are qualified to evaluate him to have a chance of changing the report.

The promotion board uses a promotion point worksheet to evaluate each candidate. It assigns each candidate a score from one to a thousand points, based on the following scale:

1. Active federal service (100 pts. possible).

2. Time in grade (100 pts.).

3. Performance of duty (evaluation report) (150 pts.).

4. Skill Qualification Test (SQT) results (150 pts.).

5. Awards and decorations (50 pts.).

6. Individual training and civilian education (200 pts.).

The promotion board then has the authority to award up to 250 points based on their assessment of the candidate's military bearing and appearance, speaking skills, knowledge of world affairs and military matters, basic soldiering, and potential for leadership.

A candidate must achieve a minimum score of 450 points to be eligible for promotion to E/5, while E/6 requires at least 550 points. However, the minimum score required for promotion in many MOS's (job categories) is set much higher. In each service, one's chances for promotion and even retention depend, to a considerable degree, on the kind of job he performs. A tank crew member may have a much lower cumulative score than someone who works in an administrative job, but he will be the only one promoted. The military manipulates the score requirements in order to keep job slots filled.

In some job categories where there is an oversupply of workers, the "cutoff score" for promotion is set so high that almost nobody can qualify. Army Eighth Corps commander Lt. Gen. Ronald Watts recently acknowledged the negative effect this has on morale. He told the *Army Times*, "Cutoff scores of 998 [of a possible 1,000] for promotion to sergeant in some MOS's is demoralizing. This [gives] the impression that one must be perfect in order to get promoted." Sometimes those in crowded skill fields will be encouraged to retrain for other jobs.

Each of the services operates a network of schools to train its NCO's. The Army, for example, requires that anyone promoted to sergeant attend a primary leadership development course (PLDC). A basic NCO course is offered for those being promoted to staff sergeant, while sergeants first class must have completed advanced NCO school.

Promotion to the highest enlisted ranks (E/7, E/8, and E/9) is controlled by centralized boards in the Army. Candidates are evaluated by senior NCO's who are qualified in the same military specialties.

The Marine Corp's promotion system resembles the Army's in most respects, while the Navy's is more formalized. Starting with E/4's, all sailors periodically sit for comprehensive promotion exams. These scores, along with Navy-wide requirements such as minimum time in a rating (job), occupational ability, and educational attainment, are all prerequisites for advancement.

The Air Force uses the Weighted Airman Promotion System (WAPS) to make all promotion decisions from E/5 to E/8. WAPS scores are based on time in service, performance on skills tests, promotion test scores, supervisor's evaluations, and awards/decorations.

PROMOTION OF OFFICERS

In 1981, Congress adopted the Defense Officer Personnel Management Acts (DOPMA), which standardized the promotion system for officers in all the services. DOPMA has created a system of evaluation and review that is similar to the enlisted promotion process in a number of respects.

The rules and regulations that control the promotion of officers are too complex to detail here. Basically, officers compete with each other in an "up or out" system; those who fail to win promotion must resign. For instance, captains and majors who twice fail to be recommended for promotion must quit the military. The special problems this presents for minority and female officers are discussed in Chapter 7.

ASSIGNMENT

The basic rule to remember here is that the "needs of the service" will prevail over other considerations such as personal desires. Each service member periodically fills out what GI's call a "dream sheet," in which he lists his preferences for his next assignment. Each service maintains a centralized assignment system that matches jobs to be filled with the skills, ranks, and discharge dates of GI's available for reassignment. The individual preferences of GI's are considered but are not a primary concern. In the Navy and Coast Guard, these decisions are made by a "detailer" who works on a personal basis with a number of GI's. Although it is possible to "lobby" a detailer, there are still a lot of unpopular jobs that must be filled, and some people will always be unhappy.

If a proposed assignment would pose an extreme hardship, a GI may request that his orders be delayed or canceled. Such requests are closely scrutinized and are not granted lightly.

It is sometimes possible to swap an undesirable assignment with someone who is willing to serve there in your place. However, each person must be the same rank, have the same MOS (job), and possess similar skills. Command approval is required for all swaps. The weekly *Army Times*, *Navy Times*, and *Air Force Times* newspapers carry classified ads that list swaps being sought around the world.

MEDICAL CARE

Once upon a time, the military was very proud of its extensive
system of free medical and dental care. Today, the consensus is
that the system has deteriorated badly. A growing number of military families as well as retirees have become dissatisfied with
both the quality and access to military health care.

The *Navy Times*, a commercial newspaper, published a series
of investigative articles in 1988 that documented many deficiencies. It found, for example, that the Navy has not increased the
size of its health-care staff since the 1950's, despite a steady
growth in the patient load. The total number of children and
spouses of service members has been increasing by more than 5
percent each year, while the number of Navy retirees has
doubled in the past twenty years (to 352,000) and will double
again by the end of the century.

Mrs. Cathy Smith, a Navy wife, summed up her experiences
with military health care in the Norfolk, VA, area: "There's a
four-month wait to get an appointment with an eye doctor here.
Seventy or eighty people waiting in line at the clinic is common,"
she reported. "To get a gynecological appointment, you must call
at 7:00 am on Tuesdays—no other time. Therefore, we often go to
civilian doctors, but that costs money."

Theoretically, military retirees are entitled to free medical care
at military hospitals for life. In recent years, however, many facilities have begun to place various restrictions and quotas on the
treatment of retirees. The overload is especially acute in areas of
the country like Texas, California, and Florida, where many retirees have settled.

In early 1989, doctors at the Long Beach Naval hospital told
the *Los Angeles Times* that they were refusing to accept any seriously ill patients because they feared that shortages of staff and
equipment could endanger their lives.

Vice Admiral Mike Boorda, Navy chief of personnel, acknowledged these problems in a September 1988 interview with the
Navy Times: "We know that we are in trouble . . . . Navy medicine
needs more people and more money. Military [staff] is not going
to be . . . sufficient to solve all the medical problems."

The loss of senior personnel who also serve as medical faculty
is another serious trend. As the gap between military salaries and
what doctors can earn in private practice grows, retention be-

comes more difficult. Several Air Force and Navy hospitals have been forced to eliminate medical training due to this exodus.

Staff shortages and long waits for medical care have plagued Army and Air Force facilities as well. Another quality-of-care issue is the constant rotation of patients among doctors. "The military [lacks] continuity of care," laments Navy doctor Vertrees Hollingsworth, who was quoted in the *Navy Times*. "A patient's chart is the only record a doctor sees. It's not in the long-term interest of the patient," he concluded.

The Pentagon also operates a separate health insurance program entitled "Civilian Health and Medical Program for the Uniformed Services." Everyone calls it "CHAMPUS." This program pays for most of the civilian medical bills of dependents and retirees (but not active-duty people) when the military system is unable to care for them.

An active-duty family must pay the first $100 of CHAMPUS; the military picks up 80 percent of the balance. However, with a hospital stay now routinely running into the thousands, this system can still leave a service family with a hefty bill. Retirees must pay 25 percent of their CHAMPUS bills. The restrictions and red tape associated with using CHAMPUS also have won it many critics among military families and retirees. For instance, a patient must first secure a "nonavailability" statement from a military hospital if he wants reimbursement for medical care by a civilian physician.

Because the military hospital system can no longer handle the flood of patients, it has tended to resort to private care providers who accept CHAMPUS payment. This has created budgetary problems as CHAMPUS costs have ballooned. They totaled over a billion dollars in the Navy alone in 1988.

It was mentioned earlier that the Supreme Court has ruled that active-duty GI's cannot sue the military for injuries caused by military negligence. This rule applies also to patients on active duty who are injured or killed by medical malpractice.

Recently, there have been several attempts to pass legislation that would allow active-duty malpractice victims to sue in certain cases. So far, such efforts at reform have been defeated by the U.S. Senate. Spouses and children of military personnel *can* sue for malpractice, but they must use the Federal Tort Claims Act. This law imposes a number of restrictions; for example, it denies the right to trial by jury and also prohibits punitive damages even if gross misconduct is proven.

If you suspect that your spouse or child has been a victim of medical malpractice, you should immediately contact a civilian attorney who specializes in this field. I would recommend against discussing your claim with members of the military's Judge Advocate General Corps before you have consulted with your private attorney. Lawyers often handle these cases on a contingency fee basis, meaning that you will owe nothing unless a settlement or verdict is won. If that happens, your attorney will receive a portion of the award, plus expenses.

Unfortunately, military dependants who are injured by military malpractice that occurred *outside* the United States have been barred from bringing suit by most courts. However, a federal appeals court in Atlanta ruled in 1989 that such suits could be brought. This may provide a remedy for families who can sue in Georgia or other southeastern states.

EDUCATIONAL BENEFITS

Active-Duty Tuition Assistance

Recruiters sometimes stress that the military will help you work towards a college degree while you are on active-duty. The armed forces will pay for most of your college tuition, although some service members find that their work schedule makes it impossible to take advantage of this benefit. If you belong to a unit that assigns a lot of extra duty or goes to "the field" regularly, college study will be out of the question.

In general, the military pays 75 percent of enlisted members' tuition costs and 100 percent for officers. A GI must secure his commander's permission before he enrolls. In recent years, budgetary problems have forced each of the branches to place restrictions on these tuition-aid programs. You will be denied reimbursement if funds for that fiscal year are exhausted.

A number of colleges and universities offer courses on military bases or in nearby communities. One of the largest such programs is operated by the University of Maryland, which offers undergraduate-and graduate-level courses at 200 military bases around the world. For those who are assigned to remote locales, correspondence courses are available.

To place this benefit in perspective, only 11 percent of enlisted personnel in the lower ranks (which constitutes four fifths of all enlisteds) received any tuition reimbursement payments during the years 1984 to 1988.

The GI Bill

Anyone who joined the military after July 1, 1985, is covered by the "new" GI Bill provided he chooses to participate. The only cost to GI's is an initial contribution of $1,200, which is deducted from their paychecks during the first twelve months of service. This contribution is nonrefundable, unless the GI is killed in the line of duty.

The program pays a veteran with three or more years' service a monthly stipend of $300 for thirty-six months of college study. Given the rising tuition and living costs at all colleges today, this covers little more than tuition and books at most public universities. Therefore, the veteran has to take a job or obtain substantial student loans to pay his other costs. This may explain why 250,000 GI's chose not to participate in the program during its first three years of operation.

The military also operates a number of its own schools that teach military-related subjects. Admission to these schools is highly competitive, but students receive full pay and benefits while attending them. A few examples are the Air Force Institute of Technology, the Naval Postgraduate School, the Army's Command and General Staff College, the National Defense University, and the Army's War College.

FAMILY ASSISTANCE

The military lifestyle, with its frequent moves, unpredictable work schedules, and long separations, can place a lot of strain on the family. In recognition of this, most military bases now have family support centers that are staffed by both professionals and volunteers. They provide a broad range of services from crisis counseling to job referral. Many of the centers also have 24-hour "hot lines" to cope with emergencies such as suicide attempts and child abuse. They also provide referrals to many other social service agencies such as the Red Cross, USO, and the YMCA.

THE BEST AND WORST MILITARY BASES

In May 1989, the *Army Times* newspaper published the results of an informal poll of active-duty military personnel about their most favored and most hated military assignments. The newspaper received nearly 10,000 responses, the conclusions of which are summarized below.

Best Army Bases

Fort Lewis, WA
Fort Bragg, NC
Fort Hood, TX

Worst Army Bases

Fort Polk, LA
Fort Riley, KS
Fort Hood, TX (People feel
　strongly one way or
　another!)

Best Navy Bases

San Diego, CA
Pearl Harbor, HI
Pensacola, FL

Worst Navy Bases

Norfolk, VA
Great Lakes, Chicago, IL
Adak, AK

Best Air Force Bases

Langley AFB, VA
McChord AFB, WA
Patrick AFB, FL

Worst Air Force Bases

Minot AFB, ND
Loring AFB, ME
Grand Forks AFB, ND

Best Marine Bases

Camp Pendleton, CA
Camp LeJeune, NC
Kaneohe, HI

Worst Marine Bases

Camp LeJeune, NC (It's all a
　matter of opinion!)
Camp Pendleton, CA
　(Ditto. . . !)
Twentynine Palms, CA

Chapter 5

If Things Go Wrong— Military Punishment

"The need for special regulations [for] military discipline and the consequent need ... for an exclusive system of military justice is too obvious to require extensive discussion."

—U.S. SUPREME COURT (1983 DECISION)

The American military has always used its own legal system to punish soldiers who break its rules. Originally, military officers dished out harsh punishment right on the battlefield. Slowly, this system of "drumhead justice" was changed, with military courts and lawyers taking over some of the commanders' powers. It's fair to say, however, that even today, the primary purpose of the military's justice system is to enforce discipline and to ensure the commander's authority over his troops.

The military command places a strong emphasis on top-down control as a principal means of enforcing its authority. There are various ways to motivate people to do their jobs but historically the military has preferred the authoritarian approach. A few excerpts from the Army Officer's Guide (1988 Edition) show what I mean; "One difference between a fine military unit and a [bad one] is the degree of obedience to the will of the leader. [He] has strong powers to exact obedience. The leader must detect transgressions, determine the cause and apply sound corrective action. If [the leader] habitually overlooks transgressions or lightly passes them by, he or she is lost. When the big test comes, the unit will fail to take the hill and soldiers will die who should have lived."

After World War II, the U.S. military underwent a major overhaul. The Uniform Code of Military Justice (UCMJ) was adopted by Congress as the basic legal code for all the service branches. The UCMJ, along with the Manual for Courts-Martial, defines criminal conduct and outlines the procedures that military courts are to follow.

Out of 144 sections of the UCMJ, 57 deal with specific crimes. Some of the statutes concerning rape, robbery, assault, etc., are the same as those found in state and federal criminal codes. But the military has also kept a number of offenses on the books, such as adultery, possession of marijuana for personal use, drunkenness, and homosexual acts between consenting adults, that are no longer treated as crimes by most civilian prosecutors. So be forewarned; the military has never liberalized its laws to conform to changes in American attitudes over the past quarter of a century.

The military also has a category of crimes, such as disrespect, disobeying an order, being absent without permission, and fraternization (between officers and enlisted), which have no counterpart in civilian society. Finally, the UCMJ has two "catchall" articles whose vague language for example, "conduct unbecoming an officer" and "bringing discredit on the military service") can be stretched to include a multitude of sins.

Since its adoption in 1951, many critics, including military lawyers, have complained that the UCMJ leaves too much power in the hands of commanders. For instance, the commander as "convening authority" decides which, if any, criminal charges shall be brought against a GI. He then picks the prosecutor and all members of the jury. After trial, he must review and approve any guilty verdict as well as the sentence. Each juror knows that his commander will have to approve his future promotions and assignments. The UCMJ was changed so that commanders are prohibited from considering how a juror voted in making any personnel decision. However, it would be very difficult to prove that such discrimination had occurred.

A training manual the Army has used to teach ROTC officers about the military justice system states that the UCMJ "left the commander essentially in control of the court-martial machinery."

Congress has tried in other ways to reduce unlawful "command influence" over the system. For example, the UCMJ now provides that the convening authority shall not, "censure, reprimand, or admonish any . . . counsel . . . with regard to any exercise of . . . his functions." Unfortunately, it remains a common practice for commanders to transfer military lawyers who work too diligently for defendants to the prosecutor's office.

Louis Font, a Boston lawyer with thirteen years' experience and considerable success in military trial defense work comments, "There have been many dramatic changes in the U.S. military in the years I've been practicing. However, its justice system has changed the least; the highest ranking commander still rigs the most controversial cases."

One Supreme Court Justice, Hugo Black, a noted civil libertarian, wrote in an opinion that, "free countries have tried to restrict military [courts] to the narrowest jurisdiction deemed absolutely essential to maintaining discipline among . . . troops."

During the Vietnam War, the Supreme Court issued decisions that limited courts-martial to only those cases where there was a clear "service connection." In recent times, however, the pendulum has swung the other way. In 1987, the Supreme Court reversed its earlier rulings. Now, military courts are allowed to try soldiers for alleged crimes that took place off base and when they were off duty.

This chapter spells out the various ways that a GI can be punished for what his superiors believe to be misconduct. It will also suggest ways to best protect your legal rights. No doubt you realize by now that the military has a lot more control over a service member's life than a civilian employer ever has. The military will prosecute GI's for things that most civilians today would consider either harmless or nobody's business. Summarized below are the various components of the military disciplinary system, beginning with the least punitive measures and moving up the scale to courts-martial, which can impose long prison terms and even death sentences.

INFORMAL MECHANISMS

Counseling and Instruction

Military commanders, including enlisted NCO's, have the right to counsel or instruct a GI about almost anything. An unkempt uniform or a GI's failure to promptly pay his debts will be considered appropriate subjects for counseling by many commanders. Although this counseling is generally informal, it carries the implied threat that more serious action will follow if the GI doesn't heed the "advice."

Admonitions and Reprimands

Sometimes a commander will decide to warn a GI about his conduct. This places him on notice that he must change his behavior. Often such warnings are oral and no record is made. "Letters of concern," however, are in writing and can be placed in the "temporary" section of your personnel file. These letters can have a negative impact on decisions about promotions or assignments. Normally, a GI has thirty days within which to rebut the allegations in this letter. It will also state that it "is not a punishment under Article 15."

ADMINISTRATIVE PUNISHMENTS

Although these measures may appear trivial when compared to a court-martial, they can set in motion a chain of events that can end your military career. Defense attorney Louis Font observes, "These administrative actions can be very damaging, yet most GI's don't realize that they should fight them until it's too late."

Withholding Privileges

Officers can withhold permission to do things as a form of punishment. For instance, a commander can refuse to issue a weekend pass that a GI needs to go home or can deny him entry to the Enlisted Club. A commander is supposed to withhold only privileges that are reasonably related to the offense committed. For example, he shouldn't suspend someone's right to drive on post unless the misconduct concerned driving.

Reduction in Rank

If your rank is E/4 or below, a field-grade officer (major and above) has the authority to take away a stripe if he decides that you are "inefficient" in your job. He also can reduce you one grade in rank if you are convicted of a civilian offense, such as disorderly conduct or shoplifting. You must be given written notice of the reasons for the proposed reduction, and you have the right to offer evidence in rebuttal. If your commander rejects your arguments and "busts" you, an appeal of his decision can be made to his superior officer. As a general rule, however, officers stick together on matters of discipline and do not want to second-guess one another.

NCO's (E/5 and above) must be provided with a hearing before an administrative board before they can be reduced in rank. Just one nonjudicial punishment (see discussion of Article 15 on page 108) is enough for a commander to "take a stripe" from an NCO. This can have the effect of stripping a GI of his status as an NCO.

Bars to Reenlistment

If your commander decides that you're a "substandard performer," he can order that a bar to reenlistment be placed in your permanent military file. This bar means that you cannot reenlist. Common reasons for imposing it include repeated tardiness, short periods of being absent without leave, several nonjudicial punishments (Article 15's), or antisocial conduct, such as repeated conflicts with co-workers. You must be given a written statement spelling out the reasons for the recommendation. As with a reduction in rank, you can (and should) file a statement rebutting the allegations. Both the commander's statement and your's are then sent to the next higher commander for a decision.

If a bar to reenlistment is imposed, it is supposed to be reviewed every six months to determine whether it should remain in effect. If you change units, your new commander can rescind the bar at his discretion. Promotion boards, which review GI records to determine eligibility for promotion, can also issue bars to reenlistment.

Reclassification of Military Occupational Specialty (MOS)

Commanders sometimes remove someone from his designated job because of misconduct. Typical cases would be where a medical corpsman has become a drug addict or a finance clerk has been caught embezzling. This sanction is serious in the military because if a person isn't working in his assigned job, he may not be eligible for further training, promotion, or even retention.

A recent case in which this authority may have been abused occurred at the Marine Corps' training facility at Parris Island, SC. A female drill instructor (DI) had testified as a defense witness at the court-martial of a fellow DI for homosexual conduct in 1988. Apparently, her testimony upset someone because after the trial ended, she was removed from her job as a DI. This job can be an important step on a Marine's career path; therefore, this action places a cloud over the witness's future in the Marines. The ACLU has appealed the involuntary removal of this soldier from her job; at press time, a review is still pending. Needless to say, you should oppose any unjust attempt to remove you from your assigned MOS. You are entitled to submit a written rebuttal to all allegations.

Separation From Service (Discharge)

The military can discharge its service members in one of three ways. First, during the first six months of enlistment, each service branch has blanket authority to discharge any trainee whom it decides is not performing satisfactorily. Those discharged during this period usually receive "uncharacterized" discharges, meaning that the person hasn't served long enough to justify either an honorable or other-than-honorable discharge. Between 10 and 15 percent of all trainees (depending on service branch) are separated in this fashion even before they complete basic training.

Second, a military commander can initiate administrative discharge action against a service member at any time during his career. Some of the more common reasons for doing so include:

- *Misconduct.* This usually refers to repeated acts that do not qualify as court-martial-type offenses.

- *Unsuitability.* This can refer to the inability to learn, a personality disorder, etc.

- *For the good of the service.* This type of discharge is usually requested by a GI who is facing court-martial charges.

- Criminal conviction by a civilian court.

- Fraudulent enlistment.

- Personal abuse (alcohol or other drugs).

- Homosexuality (doesn't require homosexual acts).

- Conscientious objector (usually on application of GI).

As you can see, the discharge often is based on a factual determination (for example, a GI is deemed "alcohol dependent"), which may be inaccurate. If it is, you should attempt to rebut the determination with evidence to the contrary (assuming that you don't want to be discharged).

The rules and procedures governing administrative discharges are very complicated and vary from one service branch to another. There is only room here to explain the basic process; you should consult with an attorney or skilled military counselor about how to handle your particular case.

Normally, you will receive a written notice from your commander informing you of his intention to discharge you. This notice should spell out the reasons why you're being discharged. Sometimes the allegations may be vague and you may have to ask for more detail. This notice should also specify the type of discharge that the command is seeking; honorable, general, or other-than-honorable. Finally, the notice should summarize your rights to a hearing or to submit a written rebuttal.

If the command is recommending you for an honorable or general discharge, you may not be entitled to appear personally before the administrative board. Generally, only GI's who have served a minimum number of years (six or more is common) have the right to demand a personal hearing, unless an other-than-honorable discharge has been recommended. If you are not eligible to appear personally, you should still prepare a detailed written rebuttal. If you can, get supportive letters from your supervisors and other GI's to buttress your case.

Technically, the recommendations of the elimination board are only advisory, but the commander who appointed it will normally approve them.

Over the years, I have heard from a number of GI's that they were told by someone in their chain of command that their "bad" discharge would be automatically upgraded to honorable six months or a year after they left the service. My impression is that unscrupulous supervisors tell GI's this so that they won't fight their discharge. I don't know how this rumor got started, but it is totally false. There is no such thing as an "automatic upgrade" in the military!

Finally, the two worst discharges, bad conduct and dishonorable, can only be imposed as part of a court-martial sentence. The military is fond of saying that a dishonorable is the equivalent of a federal felony conviction. Although I don't think it is that bad, neither is it the kind of entry you want to have in your permanent record.

See Chapter 9 ("Getting Out") for a more detailed discussion of military discharges and the procedures for applying to upgrade them.

NONJUDICIAL PUNISHMENT (ARTICLE 15)

This system of punishment is unique to the military. It is called "Article 15" in the Army and Air Force, while the Navy and Marines use "Captain's Mast" and "Office Hours," respectively. The primary purpose of nonjudicial punishment is to provide commanders with a way to deal with minor infractions quickly and simply. This is the most commonly used disciplinary measure in the military; about 100,000 GI's have been disciplined in this manner annually in recent years.

A GI has the choice of "accepting" or "rejecting" an Article 15 when it's "offered" by his commander, unless he is stationed aboard ship—then he has no choice. Acceptance is *not* a plea of guilty; it is an agreement to dispose of the alleged offense using the Article 15 procedure, rather than taking the case to court-martial. It follows from this that an Article 15 can only be based on an offense that is spelled out in the UCMJ (and thus can be tried at court-martial). Serious offenses, however, for which someone can be sentenced to a year or more or a dishonorable discharge, will usually be referred for trial by court-martial.

If a GI "accepts" an Article 15, his commander (or another officer designated for the job) will conduct an informal hearing into the charges. These hearings have sometimes been called "kangaroo courts" since they provide defendants with very limited rights. For instance, no verbatim record of the proceeding is made, and lawyers cannot formally participate. A GI can, however, choose a representative (even a lawyer) to speak on his behalf, although this is seldom done. The accused can offer written evidence and also call those witnesses who are "reasonably available" in an effort to prove his innocence. However, the hearing officer will not require reluctant witnesses or those who are not physically nearby to testify. No formal rules of evidence are applied, so either side can bring in virtually any kind of evidence. Finally, guilt or innocence is decided by the same person who brought the charges in the first place.

The overwhelming majority of Article 15 hearings end with a finding of guilty (the same thing can be said for courts-martial). The rank of the hearing officer will determine how much punishment he can impose. Captains (Lieutenants in the Navy) and lower can give any or all of the following as punishment:

- Up to seven days of correctional custody (jail).

- Forfeiture of up to seven days' pay.

- Up to fourteen days of extra duty.

- Reduction of one pay grade (rank).

- Restriction to certain areas for up to fourteen days.

- Up to three days' diet of bread and water (if serving aboard ship).

Higher-ranking officers can impose greater punishment, such as thirty days of correctional custody, sixty days of restriction, or loss of all rank. If an officer feels that the sentence that he has authority to impose is not severe enough considering the offense, he can refer the case to a higher-ranking officer for disposition.

An offender can appeal his punishment under Article 15. Except for reductions or forfeitures of pay, the punishment cannot be carried out until the appeal has been decided. The appeal can be in writing or oral. It goes to the commander of the officer who conducted the Article 15 hearing. This officer can then reduce or suspend any portion of the punishment, as he sees fit. Note, however, that when the Article 15 is given for a crime such as car theft (which is not a "minor"offense), you can later be tried at court-martial for the *same* offense. Courts have ruled that this is *not* double jeopardy!

Drug Testing and Article 15

In 1982, the Pentagon embarked on a vast campaign to make the U.S. military "drug free." As part of this effort, every GI on active duty and every Reservist and Guardsman is required to submit to periodic urine tests. Laboratories test these urine samples for residues (metabolites) of various illegal drugs (marijuana, cocaine, PCP, LSD), which can be detected in minuscule amounts days and even weeks after exposure to the drug.

The service branches offer "self-referral" drug counseling that a drug user may want to consider. If a GI voluntarily acknowledges drug use and is accepted into the program, he will not be

prosecuted. This option should be discussed with a military lawyer in advance.

Any GI who registers "positive" on a urine test will be interrogated about drug use. Military investigators are particularly interested in learning the identities of drug sellers and of other users. A
detainee may be promised leniency in exchange for "cooperation," but most commands have a policy of punishing anyone who
fails his urine test. (See the discussion about how to handle police
interrogations in the "court-martial" section on page 114).

The urine-test program has greatly simplified the job of military investigators in drug cases. Military courts now routinely allow juries to convict service members of drug use or drug possession when the prosecution's only principal evidence is the lab
report showing a certain level of drug residue in urine. There
isn't room here to discuss all the legal issues relating to urine
tests, but you should know that military appeals courts have
ruled that compulsory testing is not an unconstitutional search.
They have also ruled that testing doesn't violate one's right not to
incriminate oneself. Courts have placed some restrictions on the
use of blanket testing where civilian workers are involved. However, where GI's are concerned, military law applies.

Since millions of GI's and reservists have been tested by now,
tens of thousands of them have been caught in the drug prosecutor's net. In 1982, 45,051 Article 15's were given for drug use,
while 6,202 GI's were court-martialed for the same offense. By
1987, these totals dropped to 24,854 Article 15's and 2,740 courts-
martial. Lab-test results played a central role in most of these
proceedings, and a substantial number of those who were punished were discharged against their wishes. Those who are not
prosecuted are required to participate in drug-rehabilitation
counseling and are closely watched for signs of further drug use.

There has been a good deal of scientific controversy about the
accuracy of the lab tests on which most military prosecutions are
based. Most of the testing is done by commerical labs, which are
paid based on the number of specimens processed. Researchers
with the federal Centers for Disease Control (CDC) published a
study in 1985 that found "significant lapses in quality control" at
13 commercial labs specializing in urine-sample testing.

The military's highest court ruled in November 1988 that the
government must pay the costs of an expert witness called by a
defendant to challenge the validity of a urinalysis test. This may
help defendants in cases where there is a legitimate scientific issue about the interpretation of a urine sample.

The military uses the Article 15 nonjudicial punishments much more frequently than courts-martial to dispose of most drug cases. From this you might draw the conclusion that the military treats drug cases with leniency. But let's take a closer look.

Consider the statistics for just the Navy for one year, fiscal 1984. That year, it reported 27,581 confirmed positive urine tests. Of these, 17,417 sailors were given nonjudicial punishment, while another 1,710 were court-martialed. However, 6,596 were involuntarily discharged. Apparently, a significant number of those who "accepted" Article 15 punishment were later tossed out of the military. Herein lies a sticky problem for anyone who is offered nonjudicial punishment due to a positive drug test.

It appears many commanders have a preference for using the Article 15 procedure to dispose of drug cases. I have interviewed a number of GI's who were told by commanders that accepting nonjudicial punishment would resolve their problem and also avoid the harsh punishment that can result from a court-martial. However, once they were adjudged guilty under Article 15, the commander immediately began to process them for an administrative discharge for "misconduct—abuse of drugs."

If a GI has served less than six years active duty, he is usually not entitled to a formal hearing by an administrative separation board, unless he is facing a less-than-honorable discharge. These restrictions change from time to time, however, and you should always check the specific regulations for your service branch.

Years ago, a single nonjudicial punishment would not have been enough to support such a discharge action. But drugs are a very sensitive subject in today's military, and a drug-related Article 15 is enough to set the discharge wheels in motion. To make matters worse, discharge papers bearing the words "drug abuse" may also create problems with potential civilian employers.

This situation means that anyone should think long and hard before "accepting" an Article 15 for drug use. Since a special or general court-martial provides a better forum in which to present a defense, it may be best to "go for broke." However, as I explain below, the stakes are much higher if you lose.

Sometimes in drug cases, the commander will initiate discharge-board action against someone whose case was neither heard by court-martial nor an Article 15. In one Navy case I worked with, a sailor was tossed out with an other-than-honorable discharge, even though his court-martial for drug use had been dismissed on jurisdictional grounds.

Deciding Between Article 15 and a Court-Martial

You should make this decision only after you have consulted with an experienced attorney and weighed all the factors involved. As I stated, if the charge is drug use, your best choice may be to stand trial by court-martial. However, in many situations the wisest choice may be to dispose of the matter via an Article 15. GI's often choose this because the punishment is less severe than what can be given by a court-martial. Also, unlike a court-martial conviction, Article 15 punishment is not considered a criminal conviction.

You always have the right to discuss an Article 15 with a military lawyer. If necessary, you should consult with a civilian attorney as well.

If you are innocent and feel that you can collect enough witnesses and evidence to make a convincing case, then a court-martial provides the best forum in which to argue your innocence. Refusing an Article 15 doesn't always mean that you will be sent to a court-martial, especially if your commander thinks that you can mount a strong defense. No commander or prosecutor likes to see cases that are sent to court-martial end in acquittal. You'll have to decide if the risk is worth it after weighing all the factors involved.

A GI has at least forty-eight hours (seventy-two hours in the Army) to decide if he will "accept" an Article 15 or not. He has an absolute right to consult with a military lawyer; however, the amount of assistance they will provide varies widely.

A Word About Military Lawyers

Military lawyers are licensed to practice by the state to whose bar they were initially admitted. For many, the Judge Advocate General (JAG) Corps is their first legal job. They are generally referred to as JAG lawyers. Advertisements that are used to recruit law students promise that as military lawyers, they will be trying cases in the courtroom while their civilian counterparts are still consigned to the law library. For clients, however, this may not be such a good deal. It normally takes trial lawyers years to become proficient litigators. You don't want to be represented by someone who's using your case for on-the-job training.

Another problem is that graduates of prestigious law schools and top students at less competitive schools can earn upwards of

$60,000 in private law firms, right out of law school. Law students who are public-service minded are more likely to go to work for a nonprofit, public-interest group or Legal Aid, than they are to join the military.

Although some JAG lawyers are conscientious and dedicated despite the pressures and restrictions under which they work, the military's legal corps has its share of marginal performers. Also, if a JAG lawyer decides to make a career of the military, he learns very quickly that promotions and good assignments are not won by antagonizing or challenging his commanders.

Civilian attorney R. Charles Johnson of San Anselmo, CA, who has many years of defense experience, described JAG lawyers as follows: "Military lawyers all work together in the same building, with the prosecutors right down the hall from the defense lawyers. Being fellow officers, it's not surprising that they tend to socialize and to treat one another as friends and associates, rather than adversaries. Their loyalties are not to their clients, but to the military. Most JAG lawyers [are] more interested in 'looking good' to their peers and superiors and in being promoted in rank, than they are in winning cases."

Under the regulations, a defendant has the right to request any military lawyer on active duty to represent him, provided that he is "reasonably available." In the average case, however, your choice is limited to those JAG lawyers who are stationed at your military installation. You should try to learn something about the reputations of the various lawyers and choose accordingly, although you won't always get your choice.

The workload of the JAG Corps is such that even the most diligent military lawyers will seldom have the time it takes to thoroughly prepare a case for trial. The workload is heavy because the military employs relatively few lawyers, given the scope of their responsibilities. For instance, the Navy has only 980 JAG lawyers to service 593,000 sailors, and nearly 200,000 Marines have only 450 lawyers to represent them. In addition to conducting criminal trials, these lawyers must advise military families and retirees on civil law matters and handle a variety of other cases, including environment and international legal claims.

JAG lawyers don't normally have access to the kind of investigative resources that can win a case through uncovering evidence or locating key witnesses. Don't be surprised if your military defense lawyer tries to get you to swap a guilty plea in exchange for what he or she says is a light sentence, even if the facts strongly suggest that you are innocent. If you possibly can, you should retain a civilian attorney who will be immune to command pressures. Unfortunately, his or her fees must be paid by you. Usually, the civilian lawyer acts as the "lead" counsel, with the military lawyer assisting him. Most civilian lawyers believe that military judges and JAG lawyers are more scrupulous about respecting a defendant's rights when he is represented by an "outside" attorney.

Be careful whom you select as your civilian attorney. If you can, ask co-workers and local attorneys for recommendations. When you meet with an attorney, ask probing questions about his court-martial experience. Some of the lawyers who set up practices around military bases are former JAG lawyers who may be psychologically unable to fight the command aggressively on your behalf. This is particularly true if the civilian lawyer is still a member of the military Reserves and may even attend monthly meetings on base. If you pick a lawyer who's a dud, it is very difficult to mount a successful appeal based on his incompetence. In 1987, however, the Court of Military Appeals did overturn a conviction where a civilian defense lawyer had failed to interview and use a crucial defense witness. When the GI was retried, he was acquitted.

A Word of Caution

Army lawyers are required to turn in their client if they believe that he intends to commit a future crime that is likely to cause death, substantial bodily harm, or will significantly endanger national security or military readiness.

Congress has tried to insulate JAG defense lawyers from command pressure by assigning them to a separate command. Army defense lawyers, for example, serve in the Trial Defense Service, which is based in Washington, D.C. The strong peer pressure among JAG lawyers that Attorney Johnson talked about still operates, however.

COURTS-MARTIAL

A Word of Caution

If the command suspects you of knowing about or committing a crime, you will be visited or called in for questioning by either military or civilian police officers. Sometimes, your commanding officer will summon you in for questioning. The guiding principle here is simple: tell them *nothing*. Investigators are allowed to use virtually any ploy to get someone to talk once he has consented to an interview. One good ploy is for the investigator to take out a "hometown newspaper release" and tell the suspect that it will be sent, along with a photograph, to inform local media that he has been named as a suspect. Of course, "cooperation" will stop the issuance of any publicity.

It's funny; everyone has seen television shows and movies where suspects "take the Fifth" when questioned to protect themselves against self-incrimination. Yet all too often, intelligent people give prosecutors invaluable information because they think they can talk their way out of trouble. Any prosecutor can tell you of cases that resulted in convictions only because the defendant volunteered information. Most efforts to help yourself by "cooperating" will only dig you in deeper. Don't think that you can outsmart them. You are a rank amateur when it comes to matching wits with a skilled interrogator. Besides, you're scared and on unfamiliar ground.

Please don't think that there is anything unpatriotic or cowardly about choosing to remain silent. The Bill of Rights of our Constitution guarantees that no citizen can be forced to give testimony against himself. This is an important hallmark of a free society and helps prevent the use of torture to extort confessions. The Fifth Amendment to the Constitution and Article 31 of the UCMJ both protect GI's against involuntary self-incrimination. Article 31 reads in part: "No one subject to [the UCMJ] may compel any person to incriminate himself or to answer any question . . . which may tend to incriminate him."

Sometimes an investigator will try to bait you if you refuse to answer his questions. He'll tell you that innocent people are only too happy to give their version of events. Don't fall for this; remain silent. Technically, if you are a suspect, Article 31 requires the military police to inform you of your right to remain silent, that any statement you make can be used against you, and that you have the right to consult with a lawyer.

This is not to suggest that there are never times when it will be desirable to cooperate with investigators. On the contrary, sometimes it will be your best choice. However, such cooperation should always be arranged under the auspices of your attorney.

Sometimes your commander or military investigators will ask you to talk with a military doctor or psychologist about matters under investigation. You must be careful here because the usual doctor-patient confidentiality privilege that civilians enjoy doesn't always apply in the military. In some branches of the service, doctors are required to report to higher authorities what their patients tell them about their "crimes."

Assuming that you have been accused of a serious crime or that you have decided to face trial rather than accept a nonjudicial punishment, there are three kinds of courts-martial that you should know about; summary, special, and general. Their distinctive features are outlined below.

Summary Court-Martial

This court is the simplest and most informal proceeding of the three. It operates like an Article 15 hearing in that one officer (sometimes, but not always, a lawyer) acts as judge, prosecutor, defense counsel, jury, and court reporter. The Supreme Court ruled some years ago that the military doesn't have to provide defendants with lawyers at summary courts. Also, a defendant will not normally be allowed to use an attorney that he has hired on his own.

Although a summary court does not offer much in the way of due-process protections, it can only do limited damage in terms of sentence. Maximum penalties are thirty days of confinement, forty-five days of hard labor, sixty days of restriction, forfeiture of two-thirds pay for one month, or reduction to the lowest rank.

Like with an Article 15, a GI must consent to be tried by this court. If he doesn't, he will be taking his chances at the next higher level—a special court. This may be a big roll of the dice, however, since a special court can impose much stiffer sentences, as explained below. You should consult with a competent, experienced lawyer before deciding whether to be tried by a summary or special court.

Special Court-Martial

This court begins to resemble a civilian court. The trial is usually conducted by a military judge who is a trained lawyer, and you must be represented by an assigned military defense counsel. You can choose to be tried either by a three-member jury (usually all career officers) or by a judge alone.

A special court can give a maximum sentence of six months of prison, forfeiture of two-third's pay for six months, reduction to the lowest enlisted rank, or a bad-conduct discharge. If the judge is not a military lawyer, then he cannot impose a bad conduct discharge. However, if the sentence does not include a bad-conduct discharge, then the military isn't required to provide a verbatim trial transcript. Instead, the defendant receives only a summarized record that may be only a few pages long. This makes it much more difficult to argue legal points on appeal.

As you might expect, the convening authority for a special court must be of a higher rank (brigade or regimental commander, commander of a ship, etc.) than one who can call a summary court. General courts-martial, being the most important court, require convening by the commander of a military installation, headquarters, or corps.

General Court-Martial

This court is reserved for hearing what the military regards as serious offenses. In the military, however, this does not just mean serious crimes like robbery, rape, or murder. The Table of Maximum Punishments allows heavy sentences for such offences as "unauthorized use [of] military pass" (three years maximum), "unlawfully altering a public record" (three years), or "writing a worthless check for more than $100" (five years).

In civilian courts, except for murder cases or other crimes involving a weapon, a first offender is normally placed on probation. Military juries, by contrast, often impose near-maximum prison sentences for what many people would regard as minor crimes.

One highly publicized general court-martial during the Vietman War concerned an Army doctor, Howard Levy, who was charged with disobeying orders to teach medical procedures to Green Berets. Dr. Levy refused because he believed that the Berets withheld medicine from Vietnamese prisoners as a means of torture. Levy was convicted of several offenses, including "conduct unbecoming an officer," and sentenced to several years in prison. He appealed to the U.S. Supreme Court, arguing that "conduct unbecoming" was unconstitutionally vague, since a GI couldn't know in advance what conduct was forbidden. Chief Justice Rehnquist rejected this in a majority opinion that concluded that the military's criminal code may contain provisions that might not be permitted for civilians.

Under Article 32, a pretrial investigation must be conducted before a general court-martial can be convened. This proceeding most closely resembles a preliminary hearing in a civilian felony case.

The prosecution must present enough evidence to convince the hearing officer that the accused should be tried for his alleged crimes. Lawyers for the defendant are allowed to cross-examine the prosecution's witnesses and to inspect other evidence.

The defendant's lawyers must be prepared to fight vigorously at this hearing. An aggressive defense effort at this stage can sometimes persuade the command to reduce or even drop the charges.

Military commanders can lock up any defendant before trial if they think it is necessary to ensure his appearance at court-martial. The military has no bail system, and it is very difficult to get pretrial confinement orders changed once they are imposed. Locking a defendant up until trial makes it difficult for him to fully assist his lawyers in preparing for trial. This can also be very demoralizing, especially if the person knows that he is innocent. If he is acquitted, all the time he spent in jail is wasted.

A general court-martial most resembles a civilian felony trial. Two or more lawyers present the case before a military judge, with a verbatim transcript being taken. For the most part, rules of procedure and evidence are similar to those used in federal district courts. A jury of five or more members (depending on the severity of the offense) decides guilt or innocence. A unanimous verdict is not required, except where the death sentence could be imposed.

An unusual feature of the military system is the extensive use of pretrial agreements that fix the maximum amount of punishment in exchange for a guilty plea. Defense attorneys often negotiate such agreements with the prosecution because of the great likelihood that a military jury will both convict a defendant and impose a heavy sentence. The Navy's chief appellate lawyer told a national seminar on military law in June 1988 that 97 percent of all courts-martial end in convictions, and only 3 percent of those convicted receive any relief on appeal.

If a pretrial agreement is in effect, the military jury's role is limited to setting the appropriate sentence through a sentencing hearing. If a defendant pleads innocent, a sentencing hearing is also held after the jury hears the case, if it returns a verdict of guilty. In a sentencing hearing, both sides offer evidence about the defendant's character, work history, reputation, etc. Character witnesses are typically people who have commanded or worked with the defendant.

After due deliberation, the jury votes its sentence. If their punishment exceeds that specified in the pretrial agreement, the defendant receives the lighter sentence. If the jury imposes a lighter sentence than the agreement, the defendant gets the benefit of the jury's leniency.

Another problem with the military justice system is that it does not allow for most defendants to be tried by a "jury of their peers." Technically, an enlisted defendant has the right to have one-third enlisted members on his jury. In general, you should exercise this privilege because your peers are more likely to see things from your vantage point.

Black and Hispanic defendants' chances of being tried by a jury of their peers may have been improved by a decision of the Court of Military Appeals in 1988 that prosecutors cannot remove jurors solely because of their race or ethnic origin. However, the convening authority can still keep minority members off by simply not calling them in the first place.

In the late 1970's, the Government Accounting Office (GAO), an investigative branch of Congress, conducted a two-year investigation into the functioning of military juries. The GAO's investigators examined trial records from hundreds of courts-martial and interviewed many military lawyers and judges. In its report to Congress, the GAO recommended that court-martial jurors no longer be selected by the same officer who convened the court-martial. Instead, they proposed that jurors be drawn anonymously from a broad cross section of military personnel on a given base.

During this same period, the Army conducted a survey about military juries among its personnel at Fort Riley, KS. Sixty-eight percent of those who responded favored changing to the random selection of jurors.

Nonetheless, all of the service branches opposed the reforms proposed by the GAO, and to this day, commanders can still handpick jury members for trials that they have ordered.

After the Court-Martial

If a defendant is found guilty and is sentenced to at least six months or given a punitive discharge, the Staff Judge Advocate (SJA) will conduct a formal review and submit a summary of the case, with his recommendations, to the Convening Authority. He can approve or disapprove any or all of the findings, but he cannot overturn a "not guilty" verdict. In most cases, the SJA will rubber-stamp the decisions of the court-martial.

If the convening authority approves the conviction and the sentence, the case then is automatically reviewed by the Judge Advocate General in Washington, D.C. (assuming it's a general court-martial). It can also modify or vacate any finding of guilt or alter any portion of the sentence. Technically, convictions by summary and special courts-martial can also be appealed to the JAG, but the defendant must initiate such a review, and it is seldom done.

Confinement After Conviction

The military has no system of appellate bail, so in most cases the defendant will serve his sentence while his appeal is being considered. The convening authority has the authority to allow a convicted person to remain free until his appeal is decided, but this is not done very often. In many cases, the defendant already will have completed his sentence before his case has received its final review.

Military Courts of Review

Each branch of the service has at least one such court, which is staffed by three judges who are high-ranking career officers. The courts of review were originally created during World War I, following a public outcry when thirteen black soldiers were summarily executed in Texas one day after they were convicted of participating in a race riot.

These courts automatically review any conviction that results in a sentence of one year or more, a bad-conduct or dishonorable discharge, or the dismissal of an officer. The Judge Advocate General also may refer other cases to the courts of review if he believes that they concern an error of law. The defendant is assigned a new appellate lawyer who prepares his petition for review by the Court of Military Review for his service branch.

The military's highest court is the Court of Military Appeals (COMA), which hears appeals from all five service branches. Its three judges are all civilians, although most have had military legal backgrounds. They are appointed by the President and serve 15-year terms. With a few exceptions, COMA decides what decisions it will review. Like the U.S. Supreme Court, it grants review to only a small fraction of the cases that request it. Although COMA has the authority to issue extraordinary writs to protect constitutional rights or to prevent irreparable harm, the court rarely is willing to grant them.

COMA was the ultimate authority on review of court-martial decisions until 1984, when Congress changed the law to allow some service members to appeal certain cases to the U.S. Supreme Court.

Chapter 6

Foreign Duty

The number of GI's and their dependents stationed outside the mainland United States is enormous. In 1988, over 500,000 service members were serving abroad—about one in every four persons on active duty. This doesn't include the 250,000 sailors aboard ship or the nearly 50,000 GI's who are transferring from one base to another at any given time.

The total number of spouses and children who live abroad with military members almost equals that of GI's, making a total of 1 million Americans living outside the continental United States. They are stationed at 375 major bases and hundreds of minor facilities in 35 foreign countries. It has been estimated that these forces cost about $90 billion annually, nearly one third of the defense budget.

For many enlisted people, an overseas assignment will be the first time that they have traveled abroad. Unlike other Americans, whose foreign journeys often consist of a two-week guided tour, GI's and their families venture forth to deal with foreign lands and languages for two or three years.

Whether or not you are assigned abroad will depend largely on the kind of military work you do. If you are in combat arms, military intelligence, or on the flight line, you are a likely candidate for foreign duty during your first term of enlistment. Most GI's who stay in until they qualify for a pension (at least 20 years) will spend at least six years on foreign duty.

Some military families will tell you that foreign assignments were the highlight of their military careers. Others return home feeling as though they have survived an ordeal. There is no doubt that living in a foreign country with its own language and culture can be a difficult adjustment. People who are outgoing and adventurous probably have the easiest time.

Living conditions abroad also have changed a lot in the last 20 years or so. It used to be that American service members found life abroad cheaper than in the States. Their dollars went a long way in Europe and Japan, allowing them more luxuries and travel experiences than they could afford at home.

This situation has changed dramatically, especially in Japan and Western Europe. Japan, West Germany, and Korea each have risen from the ruins of past wars to become formidable economic rivals to the United States. As their economies have boomed, the dollar has declined relative to their currencies. Enlisted GI's today, especially in the lower ranks, must struggle just to pay for basic necessities in Japan and Germany.

Another important change has been the recent thaw in the "cold war" between the Soviet bloc and the West. Soviet leader Mikhail Gorbachev has expanded democratic freedoms ("glasnost") and is trying to reform the state-controlled economy ("perestroika"). These changes have sparked movements for democratic reform and restructuring throughout all of the Soviet-bloc countries, including East Germany, Czechoslovakia, Poland, Bulgaria, and Romania.

Over time, these sweeping changes will likely lead to substantial reductions in the number of American troops stationed in Western Europe. The Soviets have already made unilateral reductions in both troops and weapons, and further cuts will occur following negotiations with the NATO countries, including the United States.

In response to the reduced military threat from the Soviet bloc, President Bush has proposed cutting American troops in Europe by about 10 percent. Congressional leaders began in early 1990 to advocate much larger cuts, which would reduce our total troop strength there by as much as a third.

Faced with growing budgetary problems, Congress has begun to question the size of America's military commitments in Asia as well. A growing number of legislators are questioning why the United States should continue to bear most of the costs of keeping 100,000 GI's in countries like Japan and South Korea, whose economies are booming—partly because they are required to spend relatively little on defense. The scope of America's military commitments throughout the world is certain to be the subject of much political debate throughout the 1990's.

Although the conditions of foreign duty vary greatly from one country to another, there are some areas of concern shared by most enlisted GI's living abroad. Some of the more significant areas are listed and then discussed on pages 124–129.

COMMON CONCERNS OF GI'S LIVING ABROAD

Assistance for New Arrivals

Each service branch maintains a volunteer "sponsor" program that is supposed to help new arrivals adjust to life at their new assignment. In the early 1980's, the National Military Family Association (NMFA), a nonprofit membership organization, conducted a survey among 4,300 military families who were stationed at twenty-eight bases in Europe. Nearly half reported that they were dissatisfied with the help provided by their family's sponsor.

Currently, the Army processes all arriving GI's and their families at the Frankfurt, Stuttgart, and Nuremberg airports in Germany. Those who already have "pinpoint assignment" to a specific base (about 65 percent of the total) will travel by bus with their dependents (if any) to a "welcome center" near their duty station. Once there, they meet their sponsor—another GI who is already serving in Germany. The lower-ranking enlistees without specific assignments are sent to Frankfurt airport where they usually spend two or three days until their orders are prepared. Apparently, the "sponsor" program for officers is more extensive. Officers are contacted personally by their sponsor before going to Europe, and arrangements are made to meet shortly after arrival. A knowledgable sponsor can be very helpful in teaching newcomers "the ropes" in a foreign land.

Many enlisted families surveyed by the NMFA stated that their sponsor was little or no help in getting them settled. Some Army posts have been experimenting with having a whole unit take responsibility for assisting new arrivals. The success of this approach hasn't been determined yet.

The Army offers an orientation course for new arrivals that covers everything from elementary phrases in the local language to local traffic laws. Two Army lieutenants whom I interviewed in Landsruhl, West Germany, in November 1988, noted that many enlisted members in their units did not attend this course. In some cases, this was due to disinterest and, in others, the local commanders were unwilling to let the GI's take time off from their jobs to attend.

Access to Affordable Housing

Language and cultural barriers make living on base even more important for GI's when they are stationed abroad. Unfortunately, the shortage of military-owned housing overseas is just as bad as it is in the United States. In early 1989, the *Army Times* newspaper estimated that 100,000 eligible military families are on waiting lists worldwide for on-base housing. Housing is normally assigned by the order of arrival and the number and ages of dependent children. On Okinawa today, Marine families currently wait from seven to eighteen months, while Air Force personnel at Clark Air Base in the Philippines normally wait fourteen months before they get military housing. At the Lakenheath Air Base in Great Britain, the average wait is just under a year.

As in the United States, military bases abroad maintain a housing office to assist GI's in locating and leasing apartments on and off post. Families arriving at many overseas posts must scramble to rent housing "on the economy," as GI's call living off post. In 1988, the Army established a new rule forbidding dependents from traveling to Europe unless the GI has a firm commitment for housing within 30 days of arrival. If housing won't be available for twenty or more weeks after the GI's arrival, the command will not allow his family to join him. This policy is designed to save the Pentagon the expense of housing families in hotels or other temporary lodgings for extended periods.

The Army in Germany recently began to develop a system of leased housing, whereby it arranges long-term housing rentals with German landlords on behalf of military families. Many realtors had been charging GI's a "finder's fee" between $500 and $2,000 just for the privilege of signing a lease. Under this new system, military families can move into civilian housing without having to make advance-deposit payments.

Employment for Dependent Spouses

The stationing of American troops in a foreign country is governed by a Status of Forces agreement negotiated between the United States and the host government. The terms of these agreements vary from place to place. In the case of West Germany, the United States has agreed to employ a certain percentage of German nationals in military jobs. Such a provision obviously affects the number of jobs available for dependents of GI's. A

Civilian Personnel Office (CPO) handles the employment of civilians at each military base.

The availability of jobs is an issue with families for two reasons. One, the high cost of living at some foreign bases makes a second income essential if a family is going to do more than just scrape by. Two, military wives increasingly have their own career and professional ambitions that are independent of their husbands'. For some of these women, the years spent abroad are lost in terms of their career development.

The NMFA survey mentioned earlier also queried spouses about employment while overseas. Over half of those who had jobs felt they were overqualified for the work they were doing. Another 25 percent reported that they had been unable to find work, despite their efforts. In most countries, the language barrier will prevent most dependents from finding work in the civilian economy. Also, the Army makes matters worse in forbidding its personnel, their spouses, and dependents from operating many types of businesses from on-base housing. This restriction on home employment applies to all the NATO countries.

In May 1989, I asked Ms. Sydney Hickey, director of government relations for the National Military Family Association, if her organization had noted any improvements since its 1982 and 1987 surveys. She felt that substantial progress had been achieved in only one area, that of spousal employment. Congress has passed legislation requiring the military to give hiring preference to military spouses for many on-base jobs. Also, spouses who work for the Pentagon abroad now enjoy transfer rights to other government jobs when they return home. Hickey feels that these reforms have greatly alleviated job shortages for military spouses.

Ms. Hickey also saw some progress in one other area; dependent's schools. She expressed optimism that the new leadership was committed to improving the system after "fifteen years of stagnation."

In the other areas—inadequate assistance for new arrivals, housing shortages, high living costs, and social isolation—NMFA feels that the problems noted in their surveys continue unabated.

Cost of Living

Living costs are highest in Japan/Okinawa, West Germany, and Hawaii. In some countries, such as the Philippines, Spain, and

Greece, the local prices are still bargains to GI's. One source of relief from high prices is the extensive PX/commissary system the military operates at all its major bases throughout the world. One market research study conducted at Army and Navy stores in 1988 found that, on average, their prices were 25 percent lower than at civilian stores. However, the range of available products is sometimes a problem. In the NMFA survey, for instance, 54 percent of the respondents felt that the stores didn't carry a majority of the items they needed.

Because GI's stationed abroad are paid in dollars, the exchange rate for the local currency has a big impact on purchasing power. GI's used to receive a very favorable exchange rate that was subsidized by the military. In the late 1960's, this practice was ended and GI's were left with the same bank rate as everybody else. In 1985, for example, a dollar bought 3.5 German marks. By the end of 1988 the rate had dropped by half to 1.7 marks.

The military also makes special cost-of-living payments to GI's serving abroad. These subsidies are quite small, $20 or so per month, and vary from base to base and from country to country.

Schools for Dependent Children

The Pentagon operates 273 schools in 19 different countries with a total of 154,000 students. In recent years, military families have become increasingly vocal in their criticism of the Department of Defense Dependents Schools (DoDDS). The principal complaints are that the school's faculty and curricula are often mediocre or worse. Parents also complain that the teachers and administrators pay little attention to them. Some years ago, Congress created School Advisory Committees in an attempt to give parents a voice, but most parents believe they still lack any influence.

Another complaint is that school quality varies greatly from base to base. The *Army Times* recently reported that the DoDDS high school in Frankfurt, West Germany, offered honors classes in biology, astronomy, and physics, while students at Baumholder had no honors courses and only half as many courses to choose from.

A Congressional subcommittee conducted hearings on the quality of DoDDS Schools in October 1988. A spokesperson for the NMFA testified that the system was "neither responsive nor accountable to parents." She observed that there was no reliable system for evaluating teachers and that it was nearly impossible to get rid of incompetents. She charged that DoDDS administrators jokingly call their shuffling of failed teachers from one school to another "the dance of the lemons."

A source within the DoDDS teachers' union believes that critics are exaggerating the system's deficiencies. "These schools are no better or worse than your typical American public school," he observed. Student performance on the Scholastic Aptitude Test (SAT) tends to support this view. DoDDS students scores on both the verbal and math portions of this test have been slightly above the average score for all American students.

Adaptation to Host Country and "Culture Shock"

The extent to which GI's and their families experience shock and isolation will depend both on the "foreignness" of the host country and the service family's age, education, and social experience. Young Army officers I interviewed in Kaiserslautern, West Germany, were college graduates who had diligently studied German during their entire tour. For them, living in Europe was a great adventure. However, junior enlisted personnel just struggling to stay afloat financially aren't likely to be able to enjoy ski weekends in the Alps or visits to the French wine country.

Because almost half of all U.S. personnel serving abroad are stationed in West Germany, many of the base-towns there have taken on the characteristics of American suburban life. For example, about 70,000 Americans live in the area bounded by Kaiserslautern, Landsruhl, and Ramstein—the largest such community abroad. Streets in their region are lined with McDonald's, Pizza Huts, Burger Kings, and stores offering the latest videos and music from the States. Americans living in these areas can function perfectly well without having to speak a word of German. However, there are two sides to the coin of "Americanization." Anyone who has lived abroad knows that without some command of the local language, a visitor will never be more than a mute spectator. The rich experiences of another culture are largely closed to those who can't communicate with its citizens.

Military families who are assigned to remote duty stations such as Goppingen or Fulda in West Germany probably have the most difficult adjustment. Living in rural areas where English is not commonly spoken, they can't escape to the shopping strips of "little America" even if they want to.

The military does offer language courses for GI's at most foreign posts, but mastering another language, especially a difficult one like German or Japanese, probably requires more time and dedication than most GI's can commit. The two young Army officers mentioned earlier estimated that perhaps one in ten of their fellow officers spoke some German. They didn't know of any enlisted members who spoke the language.

Military families are most likely to suffer the disorienting effect of "culture shock" in countries that least resemble our own. Often they are shocked by the grinding poverty in which most people live in Third World countries like the Philippines or Turkey. However, they also can feel very uncomfortable in prosperous countries like Japan or Korea where the customs, food, and smells are very different from what they are used to.

In these situations, the tendency to stick close to the military post and associate only with other Americans is strong. But those who are willing to venture forth into a different culture with an open mind (and a sense of humor) will be richly rewarded.

At present, policy regarding the length of overseas assignments can be summarized as follows:

ACCOMPANIED TOURS (with dependents) 2–3 years. More difficult assignments in terms of locale, climate, and hardship will tend to be shorter; easier ones, longer.

UNACCOMPANIED TOURS (without dependents) 1–2 years. Again, the more isolated areas will require shorter tours.

IMPORTANT NOTE: The United States and the Soviet Union are currently negotiating mutual troop reductions throughout Europe. The Bush administration has proposed an agreement which would limit U.S. military personnel in Central Europe to 195,000 and 30,000 GI's for the rest of Europe. This would require the removal of between 80,000 and 100,000 U.S. troops from Europe. If a pact occurs, the length and frequency of foreign military assignments may change substantially.

FOREIGN-DUTY POSTS

A country-by-country profile of foreign-duty posts (from largest to smallest) follows.

Hawaii

Although Hawaii has been part of the United States since 1960, duty there can seem like a foreign assignment in many ways. Located 3,000 miles west of the U.S. mainland, Hawaii has been an important hub for American military operations in the Pacific since the end of the last century.

All the important military bases are clustered on the island of Oahu, the most congested of Hawaii's islands. About 75 percent of the state's one million citizens also live on Oahu. At one time, this island could be described as a tropical paradise, but not today. The NMFA, whose study of conditions on European bases was discussed earlier, conducted a similar study among 2,000 military families serving on Hawaii in 1987. The report concluded that there were several negative aspects to Hawaiian duty today.

Nearly a third of the families surveyed felt that the schools did not meet the educational needs of their children. (Note: In Hawaii, dependents attend public schools where per-capita spending for education ranks 43rd out of the 50 states).

Almost half felt that the military's medical facilities in Hawaii did not provide adequate health care.

Many families commented on the unexpectedly high cost of living and on the difficulty military spouses had in obtaining civilian employment. One fourth of the families reported that if their quarters allowance were not calculated as income, they could qualify for food stamps.

More than half of the respondents were disturbed by civilian attitudes toward military personnel that they felt were "not positive."

A shortage of on-base housing was evidenced by the fact that one-third of the families surveyed lived off base. Service members in the lowest three ranks (E/1–E/3) should not expect to be assigned on-base housing. A typical two-bedroom apartment costs between $700 and $1,000 a month. It is common to have to pay a security deposit in advance, equal to one or two months' rent.

Since Hawaii is not considered "overseas duty" (though it is as far away as Germany), military families do not qualify for benefits such as dependent-student travel assistance or home-leave travel. This means that GI's must pay the cost of this travel themselves.

One nice amenity is the 420-room Hale Koa Hotel ("Warrior's House" in Hawaiian) that the military operates on Honolulu's famed Waikiki beach. The hotel offers GI's a subsidized rate of $60 to $80 per night, depending on rank.

CURRENT DUTY ROSTER (1988)

Army   18,500 at 25th Division-(Light) Schofield Barracks, HQ, and Army Western Command–Fort Shafter.
Air Force 6,000 at Hickham AFB and Wheeler AFB.
Navy   27,500 at Naval facilities, ship and submarine maintenance ports, Pearl Harbor, and Barber's Point Naval Air Station.
Marines 11,700 at 1st Marine Amphibious Brigade–Kaneohe and Camp H.M. Smith, HQ, and Fleet Marines–Pacific.

A normal Army tour of duty (with dependents) is 36 months; without dependents, 24 months.

Hawaii can still be a tropical paradise with near-perfect weather, especially on the less developed islands of Hawaii, Maui, and Kauai. GI's, however, live on or near military bases that are in congested urban areas where the cost of food, housing, gasoline, and insurance are the highest in the United States, except for Alaska and New York City.

Alaska

Alaska has always been known in the "lower 48" for two things; cold winters and America's highest cost of living.

At Eielson Air Force Base near Fairbanks, the sun shines less than five hours a day during the winter months, and the average January temperature is 21° below zero, with 60 mph winds a common occurrence. The cost of living in Fairbanks has been calculated to be 42 percent higher than it is in Seattle, the closest U.S. city.

The military has extensive on-base housing, but if you are forced to rent, plan on paying up to $2,000 a month (including utilities) for a two-bedroom apartment. The authorized Variable Housing Allowance and BAQ are set at the highest levels in the world.

The Army and Air Force predominate here, although 2,000 sailors staff an important intelligence-gathering base on Adak in the remote Aleutian islands. This base, which is closer to Siberia (700 miles away) than it is to the Alaskan mainland, is popular. It reportedly has one of the highest duty-request rates in the Navy.

Obviously, some people enjoy the idyllic environment in which there are no civilians, virtually no crime, and pristine scenery. Actually, Adak is warmer than most of Alaska because of the Kuroshio Current that passes nearby.

CURRRENT DUTY ROSTER (1988)

Army	9,100	at Fort Richardson and Fort Greeley. Greeley is home to the Northern Warfare Training Center.
Air Force	11,000	in Flight crews serving at two bases; Eielson AFB (343rd Tactical Fighter Wing) and Elmendorf AFB (21st Tactical Fighter Wing).
Navy	2,000	serve on Adak island

A normal Army tour of duty with dependents is 36 months; without dependents, 24 months. At Fort Greeley it is 24 and 12 months, respectively. A normal Navy tour of duty with dependents is 24 months; without dependents, 18 months.

Alaska remains a rustic paradise for anyone who loves to camp, hunt, or fish. Unspoiled scenic beauty (except in oil-spill areas), rugged mountains, and dense forest will delight the most demanding nature lover. The trade-off is that one must endure a harsh winter five months a year.

West Germany (including Berlin)

This country has the greatest number of U.S. military personnel by far. Presently, 249,000 GI's are stationed there, comprising about half of all U.S. forces serving overseas.

This massive military commitment dates from World War II when America and her allies defeated Nazi Germany. In recent months, East Germany has been swept by the same historic changes that are occurring throughout the Soviet bloc. The infamous Berlin Wall, which divided the communist East from the western zones, has been torn down, and East Germans circulate freely among their West German brethren today.

Virtually all of the 250,000 American personnel troops in Germany today belong either to the Army or to the Air Force. In Germany, Army units are commonly spread over a number of bases and barracks in a specific locale. For this reason, the Army attaches the name "military community" (MC) to the principal city or town.

Currently, the major Army units are located in the following cities and towns:

Ansbach MC	1st Armored Division
Augsberg MC	VII Corps Artillery
Bad Kreuznach MC	8th Infantry Division
Bamberg MC	Various units
Baumholder MC	Infantry, artillery, armor, 8th Infantry
Frankfurt MC	V Corps and 3rd Armored Division
Fulda MC	11th Armored Cavalry Regiment
Goppinggen MC	HQ, U.S. Army/Europe, and 7th Army
Kaiserslautern MC	Various units, including Ramstein AFB
Kitzingen MC	Various units
Mannheim MC	Various units
Nuremberg MC	Various units
Stuttgart MC	Various units
U.S. Command, Berlin	HQ, U.S. Army–Berlin, 502d Infantry
Wurzburg	3rd Armored Division

The Air Force operates major air bases and facilities in the following cities:

Bitburg Air Base	36th Tactical Fighter Wing
Hahn Air Base	50th Tactical Fighter Wing
Rhein-Main (Frankfurt) Air Base	435th Tactical Airlift Wing
Sembach Air Base	17th Air Force, 66th Electronic Combat Wing
Spandahlem Air Base	52d Tactical Fighter Wing
Templehof Airport (Berlin)	7350th Air Base Group
Weisbaden Air Base	7100th Combat Support Wing

Although the American "occupation" of Germany began nearly half a century ago, the Pentagon has always been reluctant to invest too much capital in permanent base improvements. This has fed a "muddle-through" mentality at many bases. Even today, many enlisted GI's live in *kasernes*, where the previous occupants were Nazi troops. Many children attend school in old buildings that were converted from other uses. Chronic shortages in on-post housing at many bases have already been mentioned.

Incidentally, each military command must have detailed plans to evacuate all military dependents if war should break out. In theory, at least, there would be enough time to implement these Noncombatant Evacuation Orders (NEO's) before enemy troops could interrupt them.

In an effort to conserve money, personnel serving in Germany today are urged to volunteer for more time abroad. Until recently, the Army gave any GI and his family free round-trip tickets home if he extended for another three years. This reward recently was restricted to GI's who change posts within Europe when they extend.

One very pleasant fringe benefit for military personnel in Europe are the Armed Forces Recreation Centers located in the Alpine resort region of southern Germany. The three centers at Berchtesgarden, Chiemsee, and Garmisch offer a wide variety of outdoor activities from golf, tennis, and skiing to white-water rafting. The resorts are open year round and feature hotels, guest lodges, and campsites for the exclusive use of U.S. military personnel. Organized tours to tourist sites and cities like Venice, Munich, or Salzberg are also available.

A Word About Berlin

Until very recently, West Berlin was an "island city" completely surrounded by communist East Germany. Major changes in that state, coupled with the destruction of the Berlin Wall have created a much more open atmosphere throughout the city. Actually, Berlin is a very large and cosmopolitan city with many lovely parks and forests. Until the devastation of World War II and its division into two parts, Berlin vigorously competed with Paris, London, and New York as a major intellectual and cultural center. Today, West Berlin still exerts a strong artistic and intellectual influence on the West. There are probably no more than ten cities in the world that surpass Berlin in terms of high-quality museums, restaurants, cultural events, and nightlife.

A Word about Passports

If you (or members of your family) plan on visiting countries other than the one to which you are assigned, you should each obtain U.S. passports. Although some countries will permit a GI to enter with only a military ID card, dependents must have passports. As long as family members are "command-sponsored" (authorized to accompany the GI), passport fees will be waived. It is advisable to obtain these before leaving the United States. Contact a passport agency office or post office for details.

Japan (including Okinawa)

American troops were first stationed here following the defeat of Imperial Japan in World War II. Since then, Japan's post-war recovery and emergence as an economic power has been the envy of other nations. Some economists have argued that Japan's meteoric rise to world-power status occurred partly because it was able to spend its capital on the development of new technologies and industries, rather than on troops and weapons. The military umbrella provided by U.S. forces allowed the Japanese to assign a low priority to defense spending.

Even today, Japan's military consumes a much smaller part of the national budget than in other major countries. Despite the benefits they derive from the American military, the Japanese are divided over whether U.S. bases should stay or go. Much of the strong anti-nuclear sentiment among the Japanese stems from the U.S. nuclear bombing of Hiroshima and Nagasaki—the only military use of nuclear weapons in world history. The survivors of those bombings are called *hibakusha*, and they still play an influential role in the movement against nuclear weapons.

Under Japanese law, nuclear weapons are forbidden anywhere in the country. The U.S. military has never officially acknowledged that its ships or facilities possess nukes, but when reports have periodically appeared about their presence in Japanese ports, tens of thousands have marched to demand that the United States withdraw these weapons. In May 1989, the disclosure that an American hydrogen bomb had been "lost" off the coast of Japan in 1965 caused a new furor. According to former crew members of the aircraft carrier *Ticonderoga*, a Navy jet carrying a hydrogen bomb rolled off the ship's deck into the sea about 80 miles from shore. The bomb, which went down in 16,000 feet of water, was never recovered.

Incidentally, GI's who serve in Japan seldom experience any overt hostility from anti-nuke protesters. The Japanese, with few exceptions, are too polite to subject foreign guests (even unwanted ones) to rude behavior.

Japan is a densely populated country with 120 million people living in a land area about the size of California. Since three-fourths of the country is mountainous, the habitable areas are quite densely settled. Tokyo's 11 million residents make it the world's largest city.

The language barrier for non-Japanese speakers is severe. Outside of tourist sites and hotels, very little English is spoken. The pronunciation and grammar of Japanese is quite difficult. A dedicated student will be lucky if he can speak more than a few simple phrases after months of practice. Also, business and street signs if they exist at all, are often in Japanese characters, making navigation very difficult.

As with Germany, Japan's booming economy has hurt military families who receive their pay in dollars. From 1984 to 1987, for example, the yen-to-dollar rate dropped from 265 to 130. In mid-1989, the rate hovered around 140 yen to the dollar.

Tokyo is generally regarded today as the world's most expensive city. A taxi ride from the airport to the city center will cost about $100, as will a double room in a very modest Tokyo hotel. One of the two principal Navy bases, Yokosuka, is located in the greater Tokyo area, as is the Army's Camp Zama and the Yokota Air Base.

Military families need a car to get around, but this can be expensive. The Japanese government no longer permits any foreign-built automobiles to be imported. Used Japanese cars are readily available, but the cost of insurance, gasoline, and maintenance is quite high.

The majority of Marines assigned to Japan actually serve on the island of Okinawa, which was the site of a fierce World War II battle in which 12,000 American and 100,000 Japanese troops were killed. In 1972, Japan resumed control of Okinawa, which is part of the Ryukyu island chain to the south of Japan. Okinawa is about 67 miles long and is 17 miles across at its widest point. Its climate is tropical, with warm temperatures most of the year. However, Okinawa is not an island paradise with deserted beaches and unspoiled coral reefs. Over a million Okinawans share their Chicago-sized island with 37,000 GI's and their dependents.

The U.S. military has constructed several recreational centers, the main one being at Hentona. It offers many activities, including swimming, camping, fishing, and golf.

CURRENT DUTY ROSTER (1989)

In early 1990, Defense Secretary Cheney announced that as many as 6,000 GI's would be removed from Japan in the near future, as part of a global restructuring of U.S. military commitments.

JAPAN

Army 2,300 at Army HQ, Camp Zama.

Navy Atsugi Naval Air Facility (near Tokyo).

Fleet Support: Yokosuka (near Tokyo) and Sasebo (remote southwest corner of Japan; across from Korea).

Air Force 13,000 at Misawa Air Base (432nd Tactical Fighter Wing) and Yokota Air Base (5th Air Force) near Tokyo.

Marines Marine Air Station, Iwakuni (1st Marine Aircraft Wing) near Hiroshima, southwest Japan.

OKINAWA

Air Force 9,500 at Kadena Air Base (313th Air Division and other units).

Marines 23,000 at numerous Marine bases scattered throughout the island.

Japan is a prosperous and fascinating country. Although I have traveled to many remote parts of the world, including Zimbabwe, Bangladesh, and Timbuktu, I experienced considerable "culture shock" during a short stay in Japan. On the surface, Japan appears quite Westernized. In reality, it is an ancient oriental culture, with impenetrable language and customs.

Korea

Like Japan, American bases in Korea are part of the legacy of World War II. American troops were first stationed in Korea during the country's transition to independence after 50 years of Japanese rule. When hostilities broke out between North and South Korea in 1950, the United States, (along with several other countries) fought a war against the North that claimed 33,000 American lives and injured 105,000 more.

The war ended with a peace agreement that separated the two parts of Korea at the 38th parallel. A treaty between the United States and South Korea allows American troops to remain there indefinitely. Unlike Japan, there are no restrictions on deploying U.S. nuclear weapons in Korea; in fact, it is the only Asian ally that accepts them.

In recent years, massive protests led mostly by students have swept South Korea. They often are focused on two demands; *Minjoo wha* (democratization) and *Tongil* (reunification of the two Koreas). More recently, the protesters have begun demanding that all foreign troops and nuclear weapons be withdrawn from South Korea.

The military considers Korea a "hardship" assignment for most U.S. personnel. One reason for this is that only 3,000 (out of 45,000) are allowed to take their families with them to Korea. Some GI's who are denied permission take their families anyway. This can result in hardship because families that are not "command-sponsored" are not eligible for free air travel and government-subsidized housing. Currently, dependent families are allowed only at the Osan and Taegu air bases and at Army bases in Seoul and Pusan.

Because most GI's are not allowed to bring their wives or girlfriends, the military command turns a blind eye to the widespread prostitution. Large "red-light" districts (nicknamed "villes") have grown up around each of the nine major U.S. bases. Korean health officials conduct regular checks on an estimated 10,000 prostitutes for VD and AIDS.

The Army and Air Force account for virtually all military personnel in Korea. The Army maintains its headquarters at Yongsan in downtown Seoul, the capital of Korea. Most of the Army's combat units, however, are stationed at remote bases near the North Korean border. The Air Force stations its tactical jet fighters, armed with nuclear weapons, at four different bases south of Seoul.

Duty at the remote Army posts can be quite spartan, with combat "alerts" and field training taking place regularly. GI's often travel to Seoul and other cities to spend their leave time. A large hotel and entertainment complex is operated by the military in downtown Seoul. It caters to single enlisted personnel from remote duty posts, charging between $25 and $35 a night for a clean, modern room.

The cost of living for GI's is also on the rise in Korea. In 1986, a dollar exchanged for almost 900 *won*. By mid-1989, this had declined to about 650 to the dollar.

CURRENT DUTY ROSTER (1989)

U.S. troop strength in Korea will be reduced by at least 7,000 GI's over the next three years. These reductions, which were announced in March 1990, could be followed by further cuts in the years ahead.

Army   (Bases are listed from north to south, under principal town or city.)

Tongduchon

Camp Casey 8,700 GI's with 2nd Division—also HQ.
Camp Hovey 2nd Brigade, 2nd Division.

Munsan

Camp Howze 3rd Brigade, 2nd Division.

Camp Greaves 1st Infantry Brigade.

Uijongbu

Camp Red Cloud HQ, ROK/U.S. combined.

Camp Stanley HQ, divisional artillery.

Seoul

Yongsan HQ, U.S. Forces Korea, HQ, 8th Army (the Koreans want this base relocated to Seoul's suburbs).

Taejon

Camp Ames main Army nuclear weapons support unit.

A normal Army tour of duty with dependents is 24 months; without dependents, 12 months.

Air Force   Suwon Air Station   1,000 personnel at 25th Tactical Fighter Squad.
Osan Air Base   7th Air Force, 51st Tactical Fighter Wing.
Kunsan   8th Tactical Fighter Wing.
Taegu   497th Tactical Fighter Squad.

Many Koreans still remember with respect the sacrifices made by American troops during the Korean War. However, political currents in favor of democratization and against the U.S. military's dominant role are growing stronger. The presence of U.S. troops and weapons is seen by a growing number of Koreans as an obstacle to these goals. Nevertheless, the Korean and American militaries are closely connected, and a large-scale withdrawal of U.S. forces is unlikely in the next few years.

Great Britain

When World War II ended, the American Air Force units that had been stationed in Britain became permanent "visitors." At that time, the United States lacked an intercontinental bomber that could fly non-stop to the Soviet Union from the American mainland. Britain turned over five air bases in the eastern part of the country for the use of U.S. nuclear bombers.

Since then, the American military presence has grown steadily. Today, the Air Force occupies twenty-five major installations in the British Isles. These include three headquarters facilities, eleven air bases, five intelligence-collection centers, two communication centers, and four storage bases and depots. A number of other bases are kept as reserves while others are run cooperatively with the Royal Air Force. In recent years, two new bases that accommodate the nuclear-armed cruise missiles at Greenham Common and Molesworth have attracted many anti-nuclear protests including a permanent encampment of protestors at Greenham.

America's intelligence agencies also forged an alliance with their British counterparts as the Cold War set in. Several top-secret, intelligence-gathering facilities were established, some of which are staffed by Air Force personnel. One large facility operated by the U.S. National Security Agency at Menwith Hall has been described by a former NSA Director as "the world's most important communications intelligence center."

All U.S. personnel in Great Britain are Air Force, except for a small Navy base in Scotland. Given the linguistic and cultural similarities between Britain and the United States, this duty station probably offers the fewest problems in terms of adapting to a foreign country.

As with other foreign posts, the economic well-being of service members in the United Kingdom partly depends on the fluctuations of the exchange rate. In mid-1986, for instance, the British pound had declined to a point where it was trading almost even with the dollar. Two years later, its value rebounded so that it was worth almost two dollars.

In general, GI's report that their cost of living in Britain is similar to that of urban areas in the United States. Some things are somewhat cheaper, such as wool clothing and restaurants, while others are more expensive than in the States, like gasoline, imported goods, and fresh fruit. GI's who operate automobiles are somewhat protected by ration cards that allow them to purchase a limited amount of gasoline on post at subsidized prices.

Because Americans are cultural cousins to the British, most service families feel less alienation serving in England than in other countries. The Third Air Force publishes a "Welcome to England" brochure that sums it up, "Nowhere in the world has a foreign environment been more congenial to Air Force operations. In few places [is] there less doubt about dependability . . . The acceptability of Americans and their mission to the British people has been remarkable."

Minor complaints are voiced from time to time. Among them are the "wool-sweater syndrome," referring to the British practice of keeping building temperatures much lower than Americans are used to. Other peeves include the British attitude that children should be seen and not heard and a pub-closing law (10:45 p.m.) that some consider to be cruel and unusual punishment.

U.S. military courts enjoy a good deal of power in Britain, thanks to the Visiting Forces Act that prevents British courts from trying GI's for crimes that "arose out of, or in the course of" military duty. Offenses involving only American personnel or property are also left to the military's courts.

CURRENT DUTY ROSTER (1989)

Principal Air Force Bases

Since the British retain nominal authority, these bases are still identified as "Royal Air Force" (RAF).

RAF Mildenhall	3,000 airmen at HQ, Third Air Force, 513th Tactical Airlift Wing, and 306th Strategic Wing. Principal missions: transport, air refueling, and strategic reconnaissance.
RAF Lackenheath	5,000 personnel at 48th Tactical Fighter Wing, the largest U.S. air base in Europe. Includes 84 F-111 nuclear bombers; each carries 3 B-61 nuclear bombs. Principal mission: long-range nuclear bombers.
RAF Bentwaters	4,500 at 81st Tactical Fighter Wing. Principal mission: ground attack to support troops.
RAF Woodbridge	81st Tactical Fighter Wing. Principal missions: rescue, ground attack to support troops.
RAF Upper Heyford	20th Tactical Fighter Wing, 42d Electricity Combat Squad. Principal mission: long-range nuclear bombers.
RAF Fairford	7020th Air Base Group. Principal mission: aerial refueling.
RAF Alconbury	1,350 personnel at 10th Tactical Reconnissance Wing and 527th Tactical Fighter Wing. Includes TR-1 "spy planes," similar to U-2. Principal missions: fighter training/tactical reconnaissance.

Tactical Missile Bases

Greenham Common	1,700 personnel at 501st Tactical Missile Wing. Includes 96 cruise missiles.
Molesworth	Tactical Missile Wings. Includes 64 cruise missiles.

Intelligence/Communications

RAF Chicksands	1,300 airmen at 7274th Air Base Group, an electronic intelligence–gathering center.

Philippines

Recent events in this populous (50 million) but impoverished country composed of 7,100 islands have been featured on the evening news. After 25 years, the dictatorship of Ferdinand Marcos fell when a massive popular movement took to the streets and drove him into exile. Subsequently, Mrs. Corazon Aquino was elected president and promised sweeping economic and political reforms.

America's involvement in the Philippines dates from the Spanish-American War, when we won the country by defeating Spain. The Philippines is unique for being the only official "colony" that the United States has possessed.

When the United States finally granted the Philippines independence in 1947, a treaty was signed giving the United States a 99-year lease for its military bases. This treaty was later amended, and America's lease now will expire in 1991. Negotiations for an extension are underway, but domestic opposition within the Philippines could force their closure.

Many Filipinos oppose the bases because they feel they compromise Philippine independence. Others fear that they could make the country a target in the event of a nuclear exchange between the United States and another foreign power. The Aquino government must consider many factors in deciding whether to allow the base to remain, including the fact that the bases are the nation's second largest employer and an important dollar source.

The two important bases here are the Navy's huge facility at Subic Bay, adjacent to Olongapo, and the Air Force's Clark Field, near Angeles. They are located, respectively, 65 and 90 miles north of Manila, the capital. At Subic, 7,000 sailors and Marines and 27,000 Filipino civilians operate the Navy's largest logistical support base in the Western Pacific. There are nine different Navy commands, including ship repair, naval magazine (ordnance), naval communications, naval air station, naval hospital, supply depot, and the Marine barracks.

Subic Bay is an important basing port for aircraft carriers, destroyers, and other war ships that use it regularly for resupply and repair after lengthy cruises that transverse the Pacific and Indian oceans, as well as the Persian Gulf. Clark Air Field is also one of the Air Force's largest facilities in the Pacific. Over 9,000 airmen service and fly jet fighters, bombers, and transport planes.

In recent years, a communist insurgency has grown within the impoverished slums and rural areas. The guerilla fighters of the New People's Army (NPA) may pose a threat to U.S. military personnel. In the past two years, five Americans (three active-duty and two civilian defense workers) have been assassinated near the U.S. bases. Police attribute these killings to the NPA, although they have no proof. At present, a number of areas of the country, such as the Visayas, northern Luzon, and Mindanao, are off-limits to GI's due to rebel activity.

A Word of Advice

When you venture offpost, its best to stick to the tourist areas of the cities. Try to avoid drawing attention to yourself, although this may be hard for those with "GI haircuts." When I was in Mindanao in the far south, Filipino friends refused to discuss the New People's Army in public. They were afraid of both sides—the military and the rebels.

Because it is a poor country, the Philippines has a serious crime problem. Most hotels and stores in Manila (even Dunkin Donuts!) station an armed guard with a shotgun and pistol at their front door. Purse snatching, break-ins, and even holdups are fairly common, although the tourist areas seem relatively safe.

As with Korea, the military command is constantly warning GI's to practice "safe sex." Some Philippine prostitutes who have been found to carry the AIDS virus continue to ply their trade. Sailors leaving the Subic base pass a large sign posted by the Navy. It reads: "AIDS kills! Protect yourself from it."

CURRENT DUTY ROSTER (1989)

Navy	5,800 permanent party at Subic Bay and Cubi Point.
Air Force	9,500 at Clark Air Field. Includes HQ, 13th Air Force, 3rd Tactical Fighter Wing, and Airlift Wing (MAC).
Marines	1,000 for base defense and security, Subic Bay.

Panama

This tiny country dominated the world's headlines during December 1989 when President Bush ordered 25,000 U.S. troops to oust Panamanian dictator Manuel Noriega and to help install a democratically elected government that had been denied office earlier.

The presence of U.S. military bases has become an increasingly divisive issue within Panama in recent years. The country's prosperity is due largely to the fact that America needed a canal that would allow ships to pass between the Atlantic and Pacific oceans at the beginning of this century.

Until the 1960's, America's canal and its military bases coexisted peacefully within Panama. The canal brought jobs and prosperity to a region that had known little of either before. After several years of angry and sometimes violent protest, the United States negotiated a treaty that transfers complete control over the canal and its bases to Panama by December 31, 1999.

Before being overthrown, General Noriega encouraged his military units to harass, assault, and even murder U.S. military personnel. By June 1989, the harassment had reached a point where American commanders ordered that all dependents either return home or move onto the military bases. They also announced that, in the future, GI's who are assigned to Panama will go without their families.

CURRENT DUTY ROSTER (1989)

Army	Fort Clayton, Jungle Operations Training Center, HQ, U.S. Southern Command.
Navy	Naval Station, Panama Canal.
Air Force	Howard AFB and Allbrook AFB, (24th Combat Support Group).

The normal Army tour of duty without dependents is 15 months.

Italy

You might not think of Italy as an important center for U.S. military activity, but it is. America's bases were established here after the defeat of Fascist Italy in World War II. The Army and Air Force operate two bases each, while the Navy has three. Each branch assigns approximately 5,000 personnel to Italy.

The bases are widely dispersed throughout the country. The Army's bases are located not far from Florence and Venice, both premier tourist attractions. The Air Force operates bases in Italy's northeast corner at Aviano and in the heel of Italy's "boot" near Brindisi. Three squadrons of F-16 fighters are slated to be moved from Spain to a new base in either Sicily or Puglia in the near future. Two of the Navy's facilities are in more remote locales; one on the island of Sardinia and the other is Sicily, two large islands off Italy's southern coast. The Navy also maintains an important support facility for the Sixth Fleet near Naples.

Many seasoned travelers consider Italy's food, wines, and historic cities to be among the finest in the world. Service members will find reasonable prices and a good deal of English spoken in tourist centers.

Guam

Technically, this is not a foreign country, but rather a U.S. trust territory. Guam was acquired, along with the Philippines, when the United States defeated Spain in 1898. Since then, the Navy has maintained an important base on this remote Pacific island which lies 3,300 miles west of Hawaii. Later on, the Air Force established Anderson Air Base, from which thousands of B-52 bombing missions were flown during the Vietnam War—a round trip of over 5,000 miles.

Today, 8,700 GI's are stationed here, evenly divided between the two services. The Navy uses Guam as a headquarters and communications facility, as well as for ship maintenance and repair. The United States may transfer most of its Philippine operations to Guam if it is forced to abandon its bases there.

Although spending two years on an island that is thirty miles long and a few miles across is not everyone's cup of tea, those who enjoy the leisurely pace of a tropical island with great swimming, fishing, and snorkeling give Guam a high rating.

Spain

The continued presence of U.S. bases and nuclear weapons has been a hot political issue in Spain in recent years. Large-scale protests against the "gringo" bases have resulted in the United States agreeing to close Torrejon Air Base and to remove its three squadrons of F-16's during 1989.

In addition to air bases at Moron in southern Spain and at Zaragoza on the French border, the United States also maintains a large naval base at Rota, where 3,700 sailors are stationed. Located on the Atlantic Ocean near Cadiz, this base serves as an important supply and repair station for the Sixth Fleet's many ships that operate primarily in the Mediterranean Sea.

Despite campaign rhetoric that called for an end to the American bases, the socialist government of Felipe Gonzalez recently agreed to extend the base leases until 1997. It is unclear whether they will be allowed to remain after that date.

Like Italy, Spain offers great food, shopping, and hundreds of interesting tourist sites at some of the lowest prices in Europe.

Turkey

The American military has two principal activities in Turkey today. One is the operation of several top-secret communication and "listening" posts that eavesdrop on the Soviet Union. Over a thousand GI's work in facilities such as the Diogenes Station at Sinop, on the Black Sea, where they monitor Soviet missile testing and naval operations. The other is the Incirlik Air Base in southern Turkey, not far from the Syrian border. Here, 2,200 members of the Air Force spend up to 24 months in what a veteran of Incirlik described as Turkey's "armpit." Bitterly cold in winter, dusty and hot in the summer, one should avoid serving here if possible.

Greece

When socialist leader Andreas Papandreou was first elected President in 1981, he promised to expel America's bases from the country. Since then, however, he has allowed them to remain. This change was partly the result of increases in U.S. aid that reached a high of $501 million per year in 1984. It was also due to fears that an American withdrawal might prove advantageous to Turkey, Greece's mortal enemy.

In 1990, the United States closed its air base in Athens and its naval base at Nea Makri. Some of their operations may be transferred to the U.S. air base at Iraklion, an ancient city on the island of Crete. In recent years, a shadowy Greek terrorist group calling itself "November 17th" is believed to have been responsible for the killing of several Americans; some GI's have been injured in similar attacks. Military personnel should not use special military license tags, nor wear their uniforms off base.

Cuba

2,300 sailors are still stationed at Guantanamo Bay's naval base, a relic of prerevolutionary Cuba. The United States hangs onto this base today as a means of applying political pressure on Castro's Cuba, rather than for any military value it possesses.

America's claim to Guantanamo is based on an old treaty that granted basing rights "in perpetuity" (meaning forever). The base's mission continues to be support for various training activities of the Atlantic Fleet. Since access to the Cuban mainland is forbidden, sailors are confined to the base for their entire tour.

Chapter 7

Fighting for Acceptance: Women, Blacks, and Hispanics

In 1941, the United States declared war on Germany and Japan, whose armies had already conquered vast parts of Europe and Asia. Yet at this critical moment, a Congressman warned the House of Representatives, "If we take women into the armed services, who will do the cooking, the mending, the humble tasks to which every woman has devoted herself? Think of the humiliation! What has become of the manhood of America?"

Military strategists wisely chose to ignore such chauvinistic sentiments and began recruiting large numbers of women and blacks. When the war ended, 350,000 women and over a million blacks had served honorably, albeit in segregated units that were subjected to constant discrimination.

Women and minority groups have fought bravely in every one of America's wars, including the War for Independence. In World War I, for example, 34,000 females wore their country's uniform, mostly as nurses, while 370,000 blacks also served.

The story of nearly 200,000 blacks who fought to end slavery during the Civil War, only to be driven out of the military in the following decades, is a shameful chapter in America's history. When blacks were drafted to help fight World War I, some civil rights leaders publicly asked why they should fight to restore democratic freedoms in Europe that they did not enjoy at home. Secretary of War Baker refused to do anything about racial prejudice in the military. "There's no intention on [our] part to settle the so-called race question," he stated. Blacks fought World War I as they lived in America—as second-class citizens.

It was the same story during World War II. Over a million blacks were drafted and assigned to segregated units, despite many protests. Some black veterans who returned to their homes in the South after the war were brutally murdered by white lynch mobs when they refused to accept "separate but equal" treatment any longer.

America emerged victorious from the war, the most powerful nation on earth. Before long, the Soviet Union was changed from a wartime ally to a Cold War enemy. A number of factors, including the impact of America's racial practices on her foreign relations and a close presidential race in which black votes were needed, led President Truman to order an end to racial segregation in the military. One of Truman's associates later revealed that the lynching of black veterans in the South had helped convince him that change was overdue.

Although blacks were steadily integrated into all military units after 1948, another 30 years would pass before the separate status of female service members would end. They had been overwhelmingly concentrated in traditional jobs such as nursing, secretarial, and administration.

Following Truman's order, racial integration proceeded gradually, delayed in some parts by commanders who fought a rearguard action against racial change. Integration was accelerated during the Korean War, when it was learned that racially integrated combat units fought much better than segregated ones.

This chapter will discuss first the experience and problems of women in the military, followed by a similar discussion of problems encountered by black and hispanic GI's.

WOMEN IN THE MILITARY: RECENT HISTORY

The first black female elected to Congress, former Congresswoman Shirley Chisholm from Brooklyn, NY, once remarked that she had suffered more discrimination as a woman than as a black person. Although the struggle of female GI's for equality has differed from that of black and Hispanic GI's, there are similarities as well.

Congress finally consented to giving women a permanent role in the armed forces after World War II. At the same time, it set a limit for women of 2 percent of the actual force. During the 1950's and 60's, the actual number of women never exceeded half of this quota, partly because many women didn't regard service in all-female units as a desirable career choice.

While Congress was voting to restrict the number of women who could serve in the military, it was also adopting America's first peacetime draft. Predictably, only men were subject to conscription. This rule remained unchanged until the system was abolished in 1973, near the end of the Vietnam War.

The participation of women in the U.S. military in the modern era probably reached its lowest point in the mid-1960's, when only 30,000 females were on active duty in a total force of 2,687,000. Nearly all of them worked in medical, clerical, and administrative areas. Of the 6,000 women who served in Vietnam, for example, the vast majority were nurses or other medical workers.

The Big Change (1973 to the Present)

The status of women in the military underwent a profound change in the early 1970's. This was chiefly the result of two historic events. One was the adoption of the Equal Rights Amendment (ERA) by Congress in 1972. It provided that: "Equality of rights under the law shall not be denied or abridged by the United States or by any state on account of sex." The other event was the abolition of the draft and the creation of the "all-volunteer" military.

The passage of the ERA was an important moral victory for millions of women who were demanding an end to sexual discrimination. Despite the fact that the ERA failed to become an amendment to the Constitution because it was not ratified by two thirds of the states, it was a milestone, nonetheless. It declared that the equal treatment of women was now an official goal of American society.

A number of military leaders were concerned that if the ERA became a part of our Constitution, this would require major changes in the way the military had traditionally treated women. For example, it might make it unlawful to have different entrance standards for men and women.

Other issues that had been raised by the women's movement—the right to child care, birth control, abortion on demand, and equal pay for equal work—also influenced public opinion about women serving in the military.

But women were important to those who planned the transition to an all-volunteer force. They hoped that any shortages in the number of male volunteers could be alleviated by filling job openings with females.

If You're Thinking About Enlisting

You should realize that not too long ago the military was largely a male preserve. Unless a GI went to the hospital or an administration office, he wasn't likely to deal with females in uniform. Most of the military's customs and informal rules evolved from this all-male environment. Thus, when women began being assigned throughout the military, many men perceived them as a threat, not only to their prerogatives, but also to military traditions. Fifteen years have passed, but as one female sergeant told me, "the military is still a man's world."

The Government Accounting Office (GAO), an investigative arm of Congress, studied the military's assignment policies for women in 1988. It concluded that *four times* as many women could serve on active duty if the armed forces were willing to make some policy changes. "Unless the services have compelling reasons they've not [told us about], all unrestricted (noncombat) jobs should be available to men and women on an equitable basis," the agency argued in its report.

A number of other observers also have argued that some of the current restrictions the military places on women are artificial and not based on sound reasons. These restrictions place women at a disadvantage not only for enlistment but also for winning promotions and career advancement once they are on active duty.

The U.S. military operation in Panama during December 1989 demonstrates the difficulty of distinguishing between combat and noncombat roles in modern warfare. In two incidents, female soldiers actively became involved in the fighting. Two of them, who were helicopter pilots, are the first women nominated to receive the Air Medal for Valor.

The service branches require women to meet higher entrance requirements than men. They must score higher on the ASVAB test than men, and all the services (except the Marines) require that they possess a high school diploma. Recruiters usually fill their female quotas easily (except for nurses). Sometimes, they aren't even given quotas for women. This may mean that you will find it difficult to enlist at a time convenient for you or in your desired career field.

Despite these problems, American service women have made tremendous strides in the last 15 years. Today no other country's military allows women to play the central role that they do in America's armed forces. For instance, there are only ten thousand women serving in the huge four million-plus Soviet military today.

During the 1970's, a number of officer-training programs were opened to women for the first time. After some initial foot dragging, the four service academies—West Point, Annapolis, Air Force, and Coast Guard—admitted their first female cadets in 1976. In keeping with the spirit of change, the Air Force was the first to enroll women into its ROTC units in 1969. Within three years, the Army and Navy had followed suit. At about this time, each service also dropped its men-only rules for their Officers' Candidate Schools (OCS).

Challenges and Limitations: The "Combat Exclusion Rule"

Women are not allowed to work in certain jobs that their service branch has determined would expose them to direct combat or to a significant risk of hostile fire or capture. There is no single statute clearly defining those jobs that are combat related. Each service branch has developed its own interpretation of the rule, and there are many inconsistencies. For example, the Marines don't allow women to fly helicopters, while both the Army and Navy have many female "chopper" pilots. The Coast Guard places women in command of its cutters, while the Navy prohibits women from doing the same thing aboard its destroyers and frigates.

Since 1973, these rules have been subject to constant change. In general, the trend has been to open up more and more military jobs to women. Some Congressional staff members told me that the Pentagon quietly accepts these restrictions, and that Congress might vote to abolish them if the Joint Chiefs of Staff would take a public position against them.

Some military analysts have challenged rules that seek to protect women from the hazards of combat as being outdated. The U.S. military teaches its commanders that the current Soviet doctrine is to fight in a much larger war zone than was used in previous wars. They study a top Soviet military leader, Marshal Ogarbov, who has written, "The basic operation is no longer the front . . . or even a group of fronts, but a form of military action on a greater scale—opera[ting] in a theatre of military action." If rear areas could quickly be transformed into combat zones, then women who are assigned there in support units cannot expect to stay out of harm's way.

Combat restrictions on female soldiers are also the source of some resentment by male GI's because they appear to insulate women from the risks that the men must face. Most service women I have asked about the subject have agreed that women will be able to achieve their full potential in the military only if all barriers to combat-related service are removed.

OPPORTUNITIES FOR WOMEN TODAY

Please note that the military's rules and restrictions on women's participation are constantly changing. The following information was correct when researched in early 1989.

Women in the Army

The Army currently lists 275 Military Occupational Specialties (MOS's) open to women out of 323. However, tens of thousands of soldiers are assigned to a few of the MOS's that are closed, so numbers can be deceiving.

All jobs are closed to women in the following Career Management Fields (CMF's):

- Infantry (CMF 11).
- Special Operations (CMF 18), Green Berets, "special warfare."
- Armor (CMF 19), tanks.

A few jobs are open to women in the following CMF's:

- Field Artillery (CMF 13).
- Air Defense Artillery (CMF 16), anti-aircraft.

Only a few jobs are closed to women in the following CMF's:

- Air Defense Systems (CMF 23).
- Maintenance on Land Combat and Air Defense Systems (CMF 27).

• Mechanical Maintenance (CMF 63).

Nearly all jobs are open to women in the following CMF's:

• General Engineering (CMF 51), one job closed.

• Aviations Operations (CMF 93), only "Aeroscout Observer" closed.

• Military Intelligence (CMF 96), only "Ground Surveillance" closed.

Women in the Navy

Opportunities for female sailors have improved a lot in recent years. Until 1978, the Navy did not assign any women to sea duty, even aboard noncombatant vessels. That same year, a federal judge upheld the claim of several Navy women that this no-women-aboard-ship rule violated their Constitutional right to equal protection. This forced the Navy to seek Congressional authorization to allow women to deploy at sea. By 1982, women were serving aboard destroyer tenders, submarine tenders, and repair ships. At sea, they work alongside male sailors, but are housed in separate berthing areas. Because the Navy is primarily a seagoing branch, it is important that women receive shipboard assignments if they are to successfully compete with men for promotions.

In late 1988, the Navy further liberalized its policies by opening up thousands of billets (duty assignments) aboard its Combat Logistics Ships (CLS's) and land-based patrol squadrons to women. These include oilers, ammunition ships, and combat store vessels. Presently, women are serving in eighty-five out of ninety-nine enlisted "ratings" (Navy's term for MOS's).

At present, the following Navy jobs are closed to women:

• Mobile Construction Battalions ("mobile seabees").

• Submarine Duty.

• Duty aboard battleships, destroyers, aircraft carriers, and other ships when they are assigned to combat duty; for example, in the Persian Gulf. Women can be assigned to temporary duty aboard combatant ships when they are not on a combat mission.

Women in the Air Force

This branch probably places the fewest restrictions on what women are allowed to do. There are three reasons for this. First, the Air Force is the most dependent on advanced technology of all the branches. This means that both physical strength and endurance are less important. Second, its primary mission is to fly planes that must be supported by vast ground facilities that are often hundreds of miles from the combat zone. During the Vietnam War, for example, B-52's flew daily bombing runs from Guam, more than 5,000 miles roundtrip. Third, as the newest branch, the Air Force has had less time to develop time-encrusted traditions that get in the way.

At present, the following jobs are closed to women:

- Defensive Aerial Gunner (B-52 tail gunner).

- Para-Rescue Helicopter Pilot/Crew.

- Combat Controller (assist fire-direction, bombing).

- Tactical Air Command and Control (directing jet fighters to targets).

- In addition, female pilots are not allowed to fly F-15's, F-16's, and other jets when they are likely to engage in combat operations.

Women in the Marines

The Marines have traditionally had the smallest proportion of women serving on active duty. This is due, in part, to the fact that the Marines' primary mission is to engage in amphibious assault. The Marines' press office in New York describes the force as a "tactical machine" that is a fast-moving, lightly armed assault force trained for rapid deployment. At present, just under 10,000 females call themselves Marines, about 5 percent of the total force. Because of its heavy emphasis on combat operations, the Marines' press officer expressed the opinion that the Corps is getting close to "the saturation point" in terms of the number of women it can absorb.

A Marine Corps survey conducted in 1985 found that 53 percent of women Marines felt that sexual harassment was the worst thing about being a Marine. In 1988, Commandant Grey felt it necessary to issue an open letter accusing his male officers of tolerating mistreatment of women and setting a poor example for the lower ranks.

In late 1988, another all-male bastion fell when women Marines were assigned (over the Commandant's opposition) to embassy guard duty at some of the 141 U.S. diplomatic missions that the Marines protect around the world.

Presently, the following jobs are closed to women:

- All infantry jobs, including mortarman, antitank, and heavy machine gunners.

- Field Artillery.

- Armor (tank and amphibious assault vehicles).

- Helicopters and Jet Pilots. Unlike the other branches, the Marines have *no* female pilots, even to fly cargo or training flights. They justify this by pointing out that all their flight officers are "tactical," meaning that they are combat-qualified.

Several jobs (number in parentheses) are also closed to women in each of the following Marine career fields:

- Intelligence (3).

- Logistics (2).

- Engineering (2).

- Ordnance (7).

- Signal Intelligence (1).

- Military Police (3).

- Electronics Maintenance (3).

- Aircraft/Helicopter Maintenance (8).

- Air Control/Air Support (6).

- Air Traffic Controller (4).

Women in the Coast Guard

Unlike the other branches, the Coast Guard has no combat mission in peacetime, so it places no restrictions on where women can serve. However, the number of women involved is quite small—only about 2,000 in a total force of 38,000.

PROBLEMS FOR MILITARY WOMEN TODAY

Much of the recent publicity about military women has focused on those who fly jet planes or make parachute jumps. These assignments, however, are still the exception. Numerically speaking, the big changes in women's opportunities have occurred in communications and intelligence, electrical and machine repair, service, and supply jobs. About half of all women in the military today still are assigned to the traditional jobs of nursing, administration, and clerical. This still represents a big change, however, from the "old" military in which nine out of ten women did this kind of work.

There's no doubt that conditions have improved for the majority of women in today's military. However, many still believe that a double standard exists. "A guy can screw up and no one says a word," a female Army sergeant told me. "But let a woman make just one mistake—watch out!"

Sexual Harassment and Discrimination

There are probably few women in either the civilian or military workforce today who can't recall at least one incident in which they were subjected to harassment or discrimination solely because of their sex. I mentioned earlier that the U.S. military was mostly a male bastion for nearly 200 years. When women first began entering new career fields in the 1970's, many anguished cries were heard from men whose egos were bruised when women performed as well as, or better than, they did.

One potential advantage military women have over their civilian sisters is the military's top-down system of control. This gives the command more power over the conduct of its troops. Even if a male supervisor remains a chauvinist in his heart, he must be careful, lest any disrespect for or abuse of women be brought to the attention of his supervisors who will be writing his job evaluations and reviewing his promotion requests.

In the 1950's, the Pentagon established a special civilian panel called the Defense Advisory Committee on Women in the Services (DACOWITS). It presently has thirty-five civilian members, most of whom are female. In recent years, this body has become more aggressive in investigating alleged abuses and condemning military practices that degrade women.

In August 1987, DACOWITS conducted one of its periodic investigations, this time on the status of Navy and Marine women in Hawaii and the Far East. The panel produced a scathing report that shook up Navy and Marine commands. It concluded: "Abusive behavior [from verbal abuse to blatant sexual harrassment] continues to exist in both the Navy and Marine Corps. [Their] encouragement of a macho male image contributes to behavior that is . . . morally repugnant." The panel also criticized on-base social events that "emphasize sexually oriented entertainment in which abusive behavior toward all women is not only . . . condoned but encouraged."

The DACOWITS report described in detail one Naval commander of a salvage ship who publicly engaged in oral sex with a civilian woman, encouraged his male sailors to swim nude among female sailors, and threatened to "sell" the females to Korean sailors. He was subsequently relieved of his command but was allowed to retire with full benefits.

The following year, an all-services panel acknowledged that sexual harassment remained a "significant" problem within the military. It also concluded that "sexually offensive remarks and gestures" are still widespread.

Each service has formal regulations that forbid sexual discrimination and harassment and prescribe punishments for offenders. In addition, they are supposed to conduct workshops to sensitize men to the issues of sexual harassment and discrimination. The Army's SMART book, which is given to every recruit, devotes a page to describing the rights of women and minorities to equal opportunity. The Navy's Bluebook for sailors (1987 edition), however, fails to mention women or sexual harassment in its human-relations section called "Attitudes Toward Others."

Perhaps because of the intense publicity generated by the DACOWITS report, Army women filed almost twice as many sexual harassment complaints with the Inspector General in 1987 than they had in 1986. These complaints may be only the tip of the iceberg, however. The Army's Equal Opportunity Assessment for 1987 studied Inspector General sexual harassment complaints and concluded: "Other [evidence] suggests that the problem of sexual harassment is widespread, but most incidents go unreported [because] the victims . . . have no confidence that the chain of command will take corrective action when cases are substantiated."

What to Do If You Suffer Sexual Harassment or Discrimination

First, you can confront the offender, warning him that if his behavior continues, you'll report it up the chain of command. How much success this will have depends on the sensitivity of your higher ranking officers to these problems. No doubt there continue to be many service women who don't report sexual incidents because they fear repercussions, such as lowered performance evaluations.

The military has prosecuted some supervisors after women complained. One court-martial conducted in San Diego in May 1988 resulted in the conviction of Navy Commander John Boyar for fondling and propositioning women in his command. Boyar is the highest ranking Navy officer (equivalent to a lieutenant colonel) tried for sexual harassment. He was fined $3,600, given an official reprimand, and stripped of his seniority. It is unlikely that he will advance any further in the Navy.

Second, you can give him a dose of his own medicine. If he makes remarks about your anatomy or sexual attractiveness, you could return the favor, especially if your opinions are less than flattering. Some loudmouths may be silenced this way, but remember that such remarks could be like a red flag to a bull. First make sure that he doesn't have horns!

Third, you can file a complaint with your unit's "human relations" or "Equal Opportunity" office. Each of the services has personnel who have been specially trained to deal with racial and sexual discrimination. Sometimes their mediation can solve a problem and even change attitudes.

Fourth, you can file a complaint with the Inspector General. Unlike the "Equal Opportunity" office, the Inspector General deals with a wide variety of complaints, ranging from job safety to the theft of military property. The Inspector General also can refuse to investigate a complaint if it decides that it is "trivial." This step constitutes a definite escalation and can result in your being branded a "troublemaker," not a good label to have in the military. The female colonel who heads the Air Force public-affairs office in New York described the use of an Inspector General complaint as a "last resort."

Fifth, you can file a complaint under Article 138 for the redress of wrongs. This section of the Uniform Code of Military Justice allows anyone on active duty to seek the correction of "wrongs" by a high-ranking officer who has general court-marital authority. The only requirement is that you must have first sought relief from your commanding officer and been turned down. The officer who receives your complaint must review it and decide what action, if any, should be taken to correct the problem. He also must inform the civilian secretary of his service branch as to how he disposed of the complaint.

Last, you can file a formal request for a Court of Inquiry under Article 135 of the Uniform Code of Military Justice. If you feel that the discrimination you are suffering from is affecting a number of GI's and may be (unofficial) policy, then you might want to use this article. You are asking the command to convene a court of inquiry, consisting of three or more officers who, under the Code, can be convened "to investigate any matter." Although the court doesn't have any power to punish offenders, it can be very helpful in exposing discriminatory practices.

In my personal experience, requests for convening courts of inquiry are seldom granted, but the military does grant them from time to time. For example, the massacre at My Lai in Vietnam was investigated by an Army court of inquiry, which was headed by a two-star general.

Like the Inspector General complaint, these avenues should only be used when less drastic methods have failed and the problem remains intolerable. Filing such a request is likely to put a damper on the applicant's future with the military.

According to the book *Sound Off!: American Military Women Speak Out*, which based its conclusions on interviews with female GI's, the Air Force is considered to be the most responsive to complaints about equal opportunity for women, followed by the Navy. The Army, Marines, and Coast Guard are viewed as lagging in this area.

Promotions and Assignments for Women

The problem here is that a number of important career fields (combat flying, submarine duty, and leading combat units, to name just three) are covered by the "combat exclusion" rules and are closed to women. This means that women often cannot accumulate the kind of military experience valued by promotion boards. It would be very difficult to advance to the highest ranks in the Army, for instance, without having served in the field with combat units. In *Sound Off!*, one Navy petty officer summed up the problem: "You've got to have some sea time to make Chief [petty officer]. My chances would be a lot better if women could go on combat ships." A Defense Department study of promotion policies found that 84 percent of 25,000 female officers held the lowest three ranks, compared with 64 percent for the same number of male officers.

GI's have told me many times that chances for promotion depend, to a considerable degree, on the kind of job you are assigned to. Two young Army lieutenants whom I interviewed at Kaiserslautern, West Germany, confirmed that GI's in their units who served in the "combat arms" received promotions much faster than those with "support" or "admin" jobs.

The Army, for one, denies that women are given fewer opportunities to command than male officers. It conducted a study in 1988 that compared the military records of 2,000 female officers with those of men. It concluded that women received opportunities for command on an equal basis with men. They acknowledged, however, that in five fields—Aviation, Military Police, Ordnance, Quartermaster, and Transportation—men did receive more command assignments than women.

Army women lose out on three other lucrative programs; the Army College Fund, enlistment bonuses, and reenlistment bonuses. The first one pays soldiers up to $14,000 in *addition* to GI-Bill payments if they enlist for four years in a "critical skill," mainly the combat arms. The bonus programs reward GI's who enlist (or reenlist) in selected MOS's (again, mainly the "combat arms") with cash payments of up to $8,000. These bonuses, however, cannot be combined with the College Fund.

The other service branches also offer bonuses for enlistment and reenlistment, and they also tend to be for jobs that women are barred from doing.

Pregnancy and Child Care

Until 1976, any woman who became pregnant while on active duty was discharged, whether she wanted to be or not. After a federal appeals court held that this practice denied service women "equal protection" of the law, the military rewrote its regulations to allow expectant mothers to remain on active duty. Current rules provide that pregnant GI's are to be placed on restricted duty if their health requires it, and they receive between four to six weeks maternity leave. Most services require that the mother requalify at her weight limit within three months of giving birth.

It is estimated that about a third of the service women who become pregnant request discharge. If a woman holds a job in a "critical" skill area for which she has been extensively (and expensively) trained, her request may be denied. At present, about one in eleven female service members is pregnant at any given time. The problem of juggling work schedules to help perform the work that pregnant GI's are restricted from doing has become a growing problem and a source of resentment among some men. One frustrated Army major at Walter Reade hospital told the *Army Times* that pregnant GI's should be required to choose between discharge and taking a one-year sabbatical from the military.

Each of the services requires that single parents keep on file a "care statement" that describes exactly how their dependent children will be cared for in the event they are ordered to a combat zone or on an emergency deployment. If the command determines that a child-care plan is inadequate to protect the dependent, it can move to discharge the parent. In recent years, a growing number of GI's who give birth are unmarried. A recent Navy study in San Diego found that 41 percent of expectant sailors were single. The long-term effects of single parents trying to combine child rearing with a demanding military job has a number of high-ranking officials quite concerned.

Incidentally, you will be given a pregnancy test when you report to basic training. If you are found to be pregnant, you will be discharged for a "preexisting medical condition." In some cases, you may be able to reapply for enlistment at a later date. Also, the military no longer allows single parents to enlist if they have custody of their child(ren).

Child Care/Day Care

As the number of GI's with families has increased throughout the military, the demand for on-base day care has grown enormously. The strong trend toward mothers working outside the home has also added to the pressure. None of the services can be said to have made a priority of child care, although there are currently over 90,000 military dependents enrolled in 640 child-care centers at 408 different military bases. Still, there are waiting lists for admission at most bases. The situation is probably the worst in the Navy. A two-year moratorium on construction of new child-care facilities has left that service, in the words of one official, "desperately short" of child care. Pentagon leaders have acknowledged a shortage of at least 25,000 spaces, but given other demands on the budget, few people expect the problem to be solved in the near future.

A number of military parents have expressed concern about staff qualifications at some of these centers. In recent years there have been scandals involving child abuse at several military facilities. In one of the worst cases, over sixty children were allegedly abused sexually at the Army's Presidio center in San Francisco in 1986.

At present, Congress prevents the Pentagon from contributing more than 30 percent to the cost of operating child-care programs. This means, of course, that military parents must pick up the rest of the tab. Weekly fees range from $40 to $60 per child, still considerably lower than what urban child-care centers charge.

Even if a military base has no child-care center, each service parent is still responsible for ensuring that his children are properly cared for during duty hours.

Abortion and Birth Control Information

During the Reagan years, the so-called "right to life" lobby pushed through legislation that cut off military funding for elective abortions at stateside hospitals and clinics. More recently, they succeeded in stopping all such abortions at military hospitals overseas as well. This means that female GI's stationed abroad who choose to terminate pregnancies for reasons of their own, must travel to a civilian hospital at their own expense if they don't wish to become parents against their will. The only exception is when the medical staff has determined that an abortion is necessary to protect the mother's health.

The advent of the AIDS epidemic has probably delayed this lobby's efforts to restrict birth-control information. At any rate, service women may still receive birth-control counseling and prescriptions for birth-control items at military health facilities.

Fraternization

*"Relationships between service
members of different rank
which involve, or give the appearance of partial or preferen-
tial treatment ... are prejudi-
cial to good order, discipline,
and unit morale."*

—ARMY REGULATION ON
"FRATERNIZATION"

In plain English, this means that the military actively discourages people of different ranks from socializing or becoming ro-
mantically involved. There's an old military saying, "rank has its
privileges." This reinforces the idea that officers are socially superior and shouldn't mingle with those who serve beneath them.
The no-fraternization rule has become more of an issue today
because so many women are interspersed throughout the military. Maybe the command is worried that its young troops might
take the 1960's slogan, "make love, not war" to heart. For example, when the Air Force recently approved the assignment of
women to its two-person Minuteman missile silos, it added the
condition that both people be female.

Fraternization seems to become a problem most often when
an officer/enlisted relationship is involved. Although few people
are prosecuted solely for fraternization today, some tradition-
minded officers probably still deny promotions and favorable
evaluations to service members who date or marry across rank
lines. On the other hand, fraternization is no longer the taboo it
once was, and marriages between officers and enlisted personnel
are no longer a rarity.

Homosexuality

Women must concern themselves with this issue because it appears that anti-gay repression is directed at them more often
than at men. For many years there was a popular stereotype that
women who joined the military were mostly lesbians. This label,
of course, has often been applied to women who shunned traditional "feminine" roles and sought to do "men's" work.

A recent DACOWITS report concluded that service women
were *three times* more likely than men to be prosecuted or dis-

charged for homosexuality. It is not clear whether this difference is because more women in the military are gay or because military prosecutors are more likely to pursue cases where the suspects are female.

The relevant military regulation states that homosexuality is "incompatible with military service," and that it "seriously impairs the accomplishment of the military mission." Until a few years ago, GI's who were gay could serve as long as they were not practicing homosexuals. Today, this has been changed so that GI's are discharged simply for "being" homosexual. Louis Font, a Boston attorney, and I represented a young Air National Guard officer from Long Island, NY, who had exactly this experience.

Lt. Ellen Nesbitt had performed her job with the New York Air National Guard so well that she was promoted from the enlisted to officer ranks—not a common occurrence. However, when she was interviewed for a security clearance in conjunction with her commissioning, she acknowledged her sexual orientation as "homosexual." Lacking any evidence that Ellen's sexuality had any effect whatsoever on the performance of her military duties, the military nonetheless involuntarily discharged her, wiping out nine years of dedicated service. We sought, unsuccessfully, to have a federal court intercede to at least provide her with a public hearing and an opportunity to rebut her "unsuitability."

Currently, anywhere from 1,200 to 1,500 people are discharged from the military for homosexuality each year. Some of these people are prosecuted under the military's criminal code for sodomy, solicitation, and related offenses, for which they receive harsh sentences. In one case in which I was involved on appeal, a decorated Air Force lieutenant, Joann Newak, was sentenced by a military court at Griffiss AFB, NY, to *seven years* in prison for an off-base, off-duty affair with another service woman, who was not in her chain of command.

In recent years, some women's organizations have accused the military of engaging in "witchhunts," wherein a number of female GI's are interrogated and processed for discharge based solely on the hearsay of informers. In 1987, a number of Army women stationed at West Point were forced out despite protestations of innocence. The following year, a dozen female Marine drill instructors at Parris Island, SC, had their careers abruptly ended with discharges, although several protested that they were innocent.

One of the twelve females told reporters, "Every base I've been on has had one of these so-called 'witchhunts.' If they're going to [investigate], they need to do it on the male side of the house as well. They would have to admit that there are some gays among the 'few and the proud.' "

Today, nearly one in every three women in the military is black. In the Army, this figure rises to one in two. For these women, the issue of race may be as important as the problems associated with their gender.

BLACKS, HISPANICS, AND OTHER MINORITIES

The experience of racial and ethnic minorities in the military resembles that of service women in some ways. For most of America's history, both were barred from participating as equals with white GI's. Only in the 1950's were minority group members finally allowed to serve alongside white men, a privilege denied females until the 1970's.

Unlike women, blacks and others traditionally were relegated to mostly menial jobs or placed in combat units where they suffered higher-than-average casualty rates. When World War II began, the Navy had only twenty-nine black sailors who weren't waiters or kitchen help, causing one writer to dub it "The Great White Fleet." Not surprisingly, all of the Navy's 19,500 commissioned and warrant officers were white. The situation didn't improve much during the war. It took the Navy until 1949 to accept its first black female sailor.

Things weren't a lot better for minorities in other branches either. There were fewer blacks serving in the Army (4,000) in 1940 than there had been at the beginning of the century. Although 17,000 blacks served as Marines during the war (mostly as cooks and ammo haulers), not a single one was promoted to the commissioned officer ranks. After much debate, the Army Air Corps (later to become the Air Force) allowed some blacks to train as aviators, but they saw combat only in segregated flight squadrons. I have already described briefly the process whereby the armed forces were integrated, except for females, in the years following World War II.

Conditions for minorities within the military improved by fits and starts during the 1950's and 1960's. Perhaps the best that can be said is that minority-group members suffered less overt prejudice inside the military during this period than they would have in civilian society.

It wasn't until 1963 that the military was willing to use any of its enormous power to force civilian businesses, especially realtors, to stop discriminating against minority GI's.

On base, blacks and Hispanics found it difficult during the 1960's to win promotions and to secure assignment to highly skilled jobs. According to historian Jack Foner, "few blacks were found in the lower-grade NCO positions and fewer still in the higher NCO ranks." None of the services had many minority officers either, with the Navy and Marines having less than one black officer in a hundred. The army had the highest percentage (3.2 percent) in a force that was 12 percent black.

Let me offer a personal anecdote about the restrictions placed on blacks at the time. Although I was raised in a small city in the relatively liberal state of Michigan, the first time I ever saw a black woman working in anything other than a menial job was when I started law school at Wayne State University in Detroit in 1963. There, I encountered female administrators who were black.

A number of state governments kept their National Guard and Reserve units all white or strictly segregated until the Pentagon finally ordered an end to these practices in 1962. Even at the elite service academies, opportunities for minorities continued to be severely limited. As late as 1969, there were only 116 nonwhite students in a total cadet population that exceeded ten thousand.

Despite these problems the reenlistment rate among blacks in the Navy, Air Force, and Marines in the mid-1960's was double that for whites and about three times higher in the Army. These rates declined substantially, however, as the Vietnam War grew uglier and became increasingly unpopular.

The deep divisions that Vietnam caused in the social fabric of America were felt also in the black and hispanic communities. As the casualties mounted, with no victory in sight (despite President Johnson's vow to "nail the coonskin to the wall"), black leaders, most notably Martin Luther King, Jr., began to oppose the war publicly. King condemned a war that "sen[t] young black men 8,000 miles away to guarantee the liberties in Southeast Asia which they've not found in Georgia or East Harlem."

Many blacks and Hispanics were also disturbed by the fact that minority GI's were being killed and wounded at a higher rate than their numbers in American society. Black GI's accounted for 26 percent of American casualties, while another 16 percent were suffered by Hispanics.

The "black power" and "black consciousness" movements that emerged in the late 1960's also had a strong influence on many GI's. In Vietnam, black troopers wore "Afro" haircuits, special jewelry, and greeted each other with ritual handshakes and "daps"—an elaborate series of hand gestures. For the first time, nonwhite GI's refused to simply mold themselves to the customs and expectations of the dominant white society. Instead, they demanded that the integrity of black or Hispanic culture be respected.

All of these currents fed a raging discontent that regularly erupted into conflict against the almost all-white command in Vietnam. As the fighting there neared its peak in 1967, there were only eight blacks among 380 combat battalion commanders. Sometimes this conflict escalated into open refusals to go on combat operations. At Fort Hood, TX, over a hundred black GI's refused orders to go to Chicago for anti-riot duty during the 1968 Democratic National Convention because they were opposed to repressing ghetto blacks. A number of these men were court-martialed and jailed for their action.

Racial tension, occasional outbreaks of violence, and large-scale protests continued to plague some U.S. military bases both in Europe and the United States, even after troop withdrawals from Vietnam had begun. It took the Pentagon a number of years to understand what civil rights advocates were saying: that you could eliminate overt acts of discrimination and still have institutionalized or "systemic" racism. As we shall see, this remains a problem today, especially in the area of promotion.

Once the draft was ended and the bitter experience of Vietnam was behind it, the U.S. military was given the difficult task of rebuilding with an all-volunteer force. During these years (from 1975 to 1980), black and Hispanic participation in the military reached its highest levels. In the following seven years, however, minority enlistment declined throughout the military. For example, black participation had dropped from 22.3 percent to 19.7 percent by 1987.

Behind closed doors, some military leaders discussed whether the military had reached a "tipping point" at which, they feared, the predominance of minorities would deter white enlistment. Publicly, of course, these concerns were never acknowledged. The military began setting higher entrance standards in 1979, at least partly because of high attrition rates among first-termers, and minority recruitment began to decline. Hispanics were affected the most because they had a higher school-dropout rate than either blacks or whites. In 1985, for example, over 28 percent of Hispanic youths failed to graduate from high school, compared with 17.3 percent for blacks and 13.4 percent for whites. Hispanic membership in the Army dropped from 4.1 percent to 3.5 percent, even though a high birth rate had increased the Hispanic share of America's total population from 5.6 percent to 7.6 percent in the same years.

Nonetheless, blacks and other minorities continue to play a significant role in the military. They constitute about 30 percent of all enlisted people today, climbing to 40 percent in the Army. However, the higher you go on the rank scale, the fewer minorities you find. At the end of 1987, only 6.6 percent of all officers were blacks, with another 1.8 percent Hispanic.

The military made a concerted effort to educate its personnel about racism and to correct some of the abuses, especially in the early years of the volunteer military. In 1979, the Pentagon reorganized its equal opportunity programs and established the Defense Equal Opportunity Management Institute (DEOMI) to further professionalize the training of human-rights counselors for all of the services. Since then, nearly 10,000 have been trained by DEOMI, mostly in a 16-week course. Today, students spend as much time learning about sexual discrimination and harassment as they do about racial problems.

When course graduates return to their units, they function as advisors to the command on equal-opportunity issues. A school spokesman told me that their training emphasizes education, not the processing of formal complaints. In the Army, one equal-opportunity advisor is normally assigned to a brigade of roughly 4,000 people. Some military personnel question the effectiveness of the program today. Hal Harris, a black former Air Force Captain who worked as an equal-opportunity officer during the 1970's believes that the commitment the program once had is gone. "Today, it's nothing more than a management tool," he states.

PROBLEMS THAT CONCERN BLACKS AND HISPANICS

Promotion

Promotion continues to be a serious problem for minority personnel in all services, especially commissioned officers. The

Chief of Naval Operations, Carlisle Trost, ordered a comprehensive study of equal-opportunity practices at fifty-two Naval commands during 1988. The report paints a rather depressing picture, racially speaking, of the service branch that has the lowest percentage of black officers and enlisted pesonnel. The research team, which consisted mostly of minority Navy personnel, found widespread bias, and identified dozens of areas where equal-opportunity goals are not being met.

The study examined how fitness (evaluation) reports affected the promotion of minorites. It reached a candid conclusion: "Marine Corps, Army, and Air Force studies, which [have] revealed the existence of bias in their fitness report/evaluation systems also support [our] contention that bias exists in Navy reports." The study noted that, "all flag [high-ranking] officers we interviewed stated that bias existed in the Navy and affected minority fitness reports."

These fitness reports are written by a candidate's immediate supervisor and are given a lot of weight by promotion boards. Although the Trost study stated that enlisted personnel have made significant gains, it did not review the promotion figures for enlisted personnel, although noncommissioned officers also receive written evaluations.

Each service branch has regulations that prohibit promotion boards from considering a candidate's race or ethnic background in making decisions. The Air Force, for example, instructs it's promotion board: "[Your] evaluation of minority and women officers must clearly indicate you have afforded them fair and equitable consideration. Equal opportunity . . . is an essential element in our selection system." Yet if the overall fitness scores received by minorities are lower than for whites, then their promotion rate will most likely be lower.

Former Air Force Captain Hal Harris, quoted earlier, has waged a long battle to prove that the military's failure to promote him and other black officers is based on racism. In a letter to his Congressman discussing Harris' situation, the Air Force acknowledged that, "the percentage of blacks selected for promotion to [major, lieutenant colonel, and colonel] lags far behind that of the total percentage promoted." While stating that it doesn't know the reason for this imbalance, which it regards as a "serious" problem, the Air Force states flatly, "prejudice is not the reason."

The Trost Report mentioned earlier noted that the "most significant differences" between white and black fitness reports occurs at the lieutenant level (captain in other services). At that level, it found that minorities have a higher failure to promote. This is a critical point in a young officer's career. If he receives a promotion at this point, he will most likely stay in the military until he's eligible for retirement. The Defense Officer Personnel Management Act (DOPMA) mandates an "up or out" policy; if you don't get promoted, you will be dropped from the military.

Black officer candidates also drop out of the Navy's Officer Candidate School at three times the rate of whites.

Assignment

The Navy's survey also found that its assignment practices appeared to be influenced by racial factors. Because minority members are "overrepresented in the nontechnical fields," the report found, they advance more slowly and there is a shortage of minority NCO's in the senior enlisted ranks. For example, 33.3 percent of all Navy storekeepers are black, compared with only 4.4 percent serving in the electronic technology fields. Minorities are also "significantly underrepresented" in the fields of submarine and aviation. In summary, the report found that "minority officers are not being assigned to career-advantageous billets [jobs] ... and therefore are less competitive for future senior leadership positions."

Another researcher, David Freedman of the War Resisters League, identified similar problems with Army-assignment practices based on personnel data he received using the Freedom of Information Act. Freedman found that over half the jobs in "Administration" (51,000 total) and "Supply and Service" (48,000) were filled by blacks. However, blacks were underrepresented in many skilled fields such as Aviation Maintenance, Electronic Warfare/Intercept Systems, General Engineering, Aviation Operations, and Public Affairs.

One possible means of ending these problems would be to require the military to implement the kind of affirmative-action programs that have been required of many private employers and other government agencies. The programs, when vigorously implemented, can help eradicate the effects of past discrimination. For example, defense contractors who produce supplies or weapons for the military are required, by Executive Order of the President, to develop an affirmative-action program. If the Pentagon's equal-opportunity officers find the program deficient, the contractor can be barred from further business.

Military Punishment

According to DOD figures for 1987, blacks were tried by special and general courts-martial twice as often as whites. The general courts-martial also imposed harsher sentences on blacks; giving them three times as many dishonorable discharges as convicted whites. Hispanics received dishonorables at 1.7 times the rate of whites.

Black males are one-and-a-half times as likely to receive "other than honorable" discharges as are white GI's, while black females receive "bad" discharges at twice the rate of white women.

The rate for nonjudicial punishment (Article 15's), however, seems to be roughly proportional to each racial group's contribution to the whole; whites (50) percent, blacks (34 percent), and Hispanics (4.4 percent).

Discrimination in Other Countries

In some foreign countries, particularly West Germany, black GI's still report that they encounter overt racial discrimination at some German-run bars and discos. Newcomers usually can find out from other GI's which clubs are unfriendly toward them. Some minority GI's who have been tried in foreign courts for local crimes have claimed that they suffered from racial bias in the jury's verdict and sentence.

Remedies

I have already described several administrative and legal steps that minority GI's can take to redress wrongs (see *What to Do If You Suffer Sexual Harassment or Discrimination* on page 161). It never hurts to keep your local Congressperson informed about your efforts to secure justice; however, the degree of interest and assistance will vary greatly from one Congressperson to the next.

Sometimes GI's ask if there is any way they can use the federal civil rights laws to put a stop to military practices that are racist or sexist. The short answer is probably not. The centerpiece of the Civil Rights Act of 1964 is Title VII, which prohibits discrimination in employment based on race, sex, religion, or national origin. Other sections of the Act ban racial discrimination in access to public accommodations and in federally funded programs. These laws were adopted only after a long struggle by the civil rights movement to establish equal opportunity as our national policy.

Unfortunately, several federal appeals courts have ruled that active-duty military personnel cannot use Title VII to attack discrimination within their units. The courts have reasoned that if such suits were allowed, they would unduly interfere with military discipline and command prerogatives.

A few years ago, the U.S. Supreme Court also threw out a case where black sailors had sued their commanders for violating their Constitutional rights. The Court held that if such suits were allowed, it would, "tamper with the established relationship between enlisted personnel and their superior officers." The sailors were told to use the administrative channels already provided by the military, such as the Board for Correction of Military Records or Article 138 of the Uniform Code of Military Justice, which authorizes complaints by GI's for the redress of wrongs.

Chapter 8

The National Guard and the Reserves

The National Guard and the Reserves, two other important components of America's armed forces, have both undergone major changes in recent years. Many people don't understand exactly what it is that reservists do. For one thing, the Guard and Reserves are distinctly separate from the active-duty military, although they do work closely with it. Second, all reservists today are volunteers who undergo regular training so that they can carry out a wide range of military duties.

Reservists account for about a third of total Army personnel today and just over half of its combat forces. Eighteen of the Army's 28 combat divisions are composed of reservists. The ratio of reservists to active-duty personnel in the Air Force is even higher. They account for 37 percent of its total force, and 78 percent of Air Force personnel responsible for the air defense of this country are reservists.

There are 5,300 Guard and Reserve units located in 4,300 cities and towns throughout the United States today. (*Note*: the term "reservists" is used in this chapter as a generic term, referring to members of both the Guard and Reserves.)

People serving in the Guard and Reserves no longer are regarded as rear-echelon replacements. Today, they are equipped and trained for rapid deployment. If war should break out, many reserve units would be sent into battle even more quickly than some active-duty elements. About a third of all Army reservists train regularly with their "parent" units in the active-duty force. Over half of all Navy reservists receive similar realistic training, as do virtually all Air Force reservists.

In August, 1990, President Bush ordered the Pentagon to place thousands of reservists on active duty as part of our huge military buildup in Saudi Arabia. As many as 49,703 reservists will serve active duty tours lasting up to six months at military bases in both the U.S. and the Persian Gulf.

The National Guard can trace its history back to America's earliest days when they were colonial-era militias. These militias helped to fight the Revolutionary War for Independence and later fought on both sides in America's Civil War. Early in this century, these militias, which remain under the command of the state governors, were brought under tighter federal control. They eventually evolved into what is known today as the Army National Guard and Air National Guard.

Reserve units, which are controlled directly by the military services, were formed early in this century to supplement the active-duty forces. They were reorganized into their present form after World War II. All of the branches sent large numbers of reservists to fight in both World War II and the Korean War.

If you're debating whether to join the Guard or Reserves, you will be interested to know that, for the most part, National Guard units perform combat roles, while administrative and support jobs tend to be concentrated in the Reserves. The type of unit you belong to will determine where you'd serve if America became involved in a shooting war somewhere in the world.

The other important difference between the Guard and the Reserve has to do with their military missions. The Guard serves as a military force for both state and federal governments. Normally, a Guard unit is under the command of the governor of the state in which it is located, although Congress can vote to bring it under federal control. This sometimes occurred in the 1950's and 1960's, when governors in the southern states attempted to use their National Guard units to obstruct desegregation efforts by federal judges and officials.

Since it is a state police force, Guard members are often called to temporary duty when a serious natural disaster or civil disturbance occurs. Sometimes this can mean very dangerous and distasteful duty. For example, during the urban riots of the 1960's, thousands of Guard members were sent into extremely tense ghetto areas with orders to shoot to kill. Hundreds of civilians, mostly black and Hispanic, were killed or injured by Guardsmen as they restored order.

National Guard members also are often used to protect strikebreakers during labor disputes. Minnesota Guardsmen, for example, spent weeks policing picket lines during a bitter 1987 strike at Hormel. If you are sympathetic to unions, you may find this kind of duty hard to take.

In another infamous case in 1970, National Guard members were sent to quell anti-Vietnam protests at Kent State University in Ohio. Because of poor training and leadership, Guard members opened fire, killing several innocent students and badly wounding many others.

During the Vietnam War, both the Guard and the Reserves became extremely popular with tens of thousands of young men who hoped to avoid being sent to fight in Indochina. During earlier wars, thousands of reservists were involuntarily placed on active duty and assigned to combat units. But neither President Johnson nor Nixon was willing to order reservists to fight in Vietnam, despite repeated requests by their military advisers to do so. Each president apparently feared that such a mobilization would intensify anti-war sentiment among the families of white, college-trained men who were using the reserves to escape the war.

Not surprisingly, once the draft ended and American troops began to withdraw from Vietnam, the reserves began to have problems both recruiting and retraining members. In the early 1970's, the Gates Commission, which advised the Pentagon on how best to create the all-volunteer force, recommended three basic changes. One of the three was to upgrade the importance of reserve units in the overall military operations. The commission believed that if the Guard and Reserves were given more responsibility, it would make it easier to scale down the size of the active military. The commission's other two recommendations were increasing pay and benefits to help the armed forces compete with civilian employment, and increasing the number of females in uniform.

When the planners redefined the role and purpose of the reserves, they called it the "Total Force Concept." Essentially, this plan requires the Pentagon to incorporate reserve units wherever possible into its military operations. No longer regarded primarily as a backup force, reserve units are now equipped and trained so that they can be mobilized as combat forces within days after war is declared.

During the 1960's, reservists gained a bad reputation among their active-duty counterparts as "draft dodgers" who lacked military skills and discipline. Although some units still harbor marginal performers, for the most part, standards are higher than during the Vietnam period. This may be due partly to the fact that today over half of all reservists (except for the Marines) are prior-service veterans. No one serves in a reserve unit today to escape other military duty.

Since military spending has come under increased scrutiny in recent years, Congress has prodded the Pentagon to make even greater use of the reserves as a way to save money. It has been estimated that five reservists cost the military about the same as one active-duty GI. We have entered an era of tight military budgets. This means Congress will continue to press the military to use the least expensive force (the reserves) as much as possible.

Some independent analysts, as well as members of Congress, have questioned the wisdom of expecting so much from reserve units that have had no recent combat experience. The Brookings Institute, a "think tank" in Washington, D.C., recently published a book in which two of its experts cast serious doubt on the Army's claim that its reservists could perform the military tasks that are assigned to them.

RECRUITING

Several GI's on active duty suggested to me that joining the reserves might be preferable to active duty for someone who is not sure that he will like military life. The time commitment is much less, and it is easier to terminate the reserve contract than it is to get out of a regular enlistment contract.

When the draft was abolished and young men were no longer threatened with being sent to Vietnam, both the Guard and Reserves found it much more difficult to attract recruits. Following the active-duty military's lead, the reserves greatly expanded their recruiting force. Today, the Army National Guard has the largest number of recruiters (3,718), followed by the Army Reserve, which uses 1,900. Next is the Navy, whose 1,700 recruiters help it maintain a reserve force of 149,000. Although they have the second largest reserve force with almost 200,000 people, the Air National Guard and Reserves have relatively few recruiters. This is due, in part, to a reenlistment rate that hovers around 90 percent. The Marines and Coast Guard, with reserve forces of 43,000 and 12,000 respectively, also have very small recruiting detachments, numbering around 200 or less. By and large, these recruiters use the same sales talk and promises as their active-duty counterparts, at least as far as first-termers are concerned.

Reservists are processed for enlistment at the same MEPS as regular GI's. There, they undergo the same physical and mental examinations as active-duty recruits, and they sign an enlistment contract that is virtually identical to the one used for active duty (see Chapter 1).

Reserve recruiting is different from active-duty recruiting in one important respect. Military veterans account for only a small percentage of the enlistments obtained for the active military. By contrast, more than half of all reservists are service veterans. The only exception is the Marines, with about a third of veterans among its reserve force.

The Army allows a soldier who is leaving active duty to retain the same rank, pay grade, and time in grade if he enlists in the active reserves within sixty days after discharge. Other benefits are a $50,000 life insurance policy, space-available dental care at military facilities, and commissary and post exchange privileges (one visit to the PX is allowed for each four-hour training session).

The Air Force offers a special program called "Palace Chase" that allows active-duty personnel to transfer to its reserve units by swapping two years of reserve commitment for every year that remains on their active-duty enlistment.

Prior-service veterans account for about 70 percent of all Air Guard and Reserve personnel. Guard officials told me that, while they value the veterans' experience, they would prefer if the ratios were reversed. That is, that a majority of enlistees were new to the military. This would greatly help reduce personnel costs since inexperienced personnel enter at the lowest ranks and receive lower wages.

According to the annual report of the Reserves Forces Policy Board for 1988, all of the reserves continue to suffer from vacancies in the substantial number of military jobs. For example, the Army Reserves lists over 150 jobs that it is not able to keep filled. This understaffing negatively affects the ability of many units to carry out their operations and to qualify as "combat ready." Since reserve units employ their personnel in a limited number of jobs, recruiters sometimes must work hard to find people who can qualify for the required skills training. Obviously, veterans who have already qualified in a certain skill areas are in demand.

Recruiters regularly receive computer printouts that list the name, address, and military job of every soldier who has been discharged from the military in the previous twelve months. These people can expect to receive both mail solicitations and phone calls from various recruiters, especially if they worked at military jobs for which the reserves have vacancies.

Everyone who joins the active-duty military today signs an eight-year enlistment contract. This commitment is divided into two parts, the years the GI agrees to serve on active duty (usually three or four) and the remaining period, which is served in the inactive reserve. When a GI completes his hitch of active duty, he will be transferred to the Individual Ready Reserves (IRR), where he will "serve" until the eighth year has ended. Essentially, IRR status requires nothing of the veteran—no drills, training, or even assignment to a specific unit. As an Army Reserve recruiter put it, "This 'force' is just a computer tape in St. Louis."

Theoretically, everyone in the IRR is subject to recall to active duty if war should break out. However, since these reservists often have not been involved in military activities for years, their value as soldiers or sailors would be questionable, at best. A small percentage of those on IRR status (20,000 in 1988) do participate, on a voluntary basis, in various military training activities.

Reserve duty differs from active duty in that usually reservists are assigned to the same Guard or Reserve unit throughout their career. Only when someone moves a considerable distance away is he transferred to another unit. The advantage of this system is that reservists often develop very strong bonds of trust and friendship. One drawback is that personality conflicts and petty grudges can become magnified where there is so little change in personnel.

Another difference from active duty is that each reserve unit tends to have a specific mission; for example, operating a tactical jet fighter wing or a medical unit. An air unit might consist of a thousand members, all of whom are concentrated in twenty or thirty Air Force jobs. This can make a recruiter's life difficult. For instance, he might locate a prospective recruit with extensive experience in aircraft maintenance; however, on a different type of airplane. If he cannot qualify for any of the jobs that are open at the Air Guard unit nearest his home, he will either have to join a unit somewhere else or agree to be retrained. If a person joins under these conditions, he will usually have to qualify in the new skill area within a year. Prior-service vets who are being trained in a new skill usually study at a reserve school in their community. These classes are conducted during the weekend drill periods.

ENLISTMENT CONTRACTS

The period of enlistment for reserve duty varies by branch and depends on one's age and whether or not he has served previously in the military.

In the Army and Navy, those without prior military experience must enlist for a minimum of eight years. Veterans, however, can qualify for enlistments varying from one to six years (two to six in the Navy). These short contracts are offered to allow veterans a trial period in which to decide whether they like reserve duty.

The Air Force requires non-veterans to sign for six years, while those with prior service are allowed to sign for as little as one year.

Both the Marine and Coast Guard reserves require nonveterans to enlist for four years, while offering variable contracts to vets.

As with active-duty forces, the reserves have made a concerted effort in recent years to sign up more women. Today about 12 percent of all reservists are female. They are subject to the same rules that exclude women from certain combat-related jobs on active duty. The number of such jobs, however, has been declining steadily in recent years.

INDUCEMENTS/BENEFITS

As a means of attracting recruits, the reserves operate certain benefit programs that resemble those offered to active-duty GI's.

GI Bill/Educational Assistance

This benefit provides up to $140 per month, provided a reservist is enrolled in an accredited college or vocational school. Unlike active duty personnel, reservists can begin drawing GI Bill payments just six months after they begin service. Many state governments also provide additional college aid or tuition discounts to state residents who belong to their Army or Air National Guard units.

Enlistment Bonuses

Each of the reserves offers cash payments of up to $2,500 as a reward for enlisting in certain skilled jobs. There are relatively few jobs that qualify for these payments.

Federal Loan Forgiveness Program

College students or graduates who enlist may qualify to have part of their federal student loans repaid as a bonus for joining the reserves. Loan forgiveness cannot exceed 15 percent of the total sum owed each year. People who choose to participate in this program do not qualify for GI Bill payments.

BASIC AND ADVANCED TRAINING

Everyone who joins the reserves without prior military service is required to complete both basic and advanced training before they begin local duty. This means that recruits should plan on being away from home for as long as five to six months. All reservists are trained at the same military facilities as active-duty GI's.

There are federal laws that protect reservists from job discrimination that may result from their reserve commitments. The Veterans Reemployment Rights Law prevents employers from discriminating against workers who take time off to attend reserve drills or training. Reservists are entitled to return to their old job (or an equivalent one) when they return, no matter how long the training period lasts. Many states also have laws that protect Guard members from employer bias.

The federal law does not provide unlimited protection, however. A federal appeals court in Philadelphia ruled in May 1989 that employers do not have to automatically approve every reservist's request for time off. It sent the case back to the trial court for a determination as to whether a transit worker's request was an "unreasonable" inconvenience to his employer. The reserves have also developed a voluntary organization, Employer Support of the Guard and Reserve, which works to encourage a cooperative attitude on the part of employers. A Rand Corporation study of reservists who quit the military found that 31 percent gave "conflict with their civilian job" as the principal reason for leaving.

Apparently a large number of reservists continue to have problems with their bosses about taking time off for training. A special "ombudsman's" office, which has been established to help resolve individual problems, received a record number of inquiries from reservists in 1988 (6,194). Call toll free 1-800-336-4590 to get assistance.

Once recruits arrive at basic or advanced training, they are mixed into training units alongside active-duty personnel. Basic training lasts from six to thirteen weeks, depending on the branch of service. After that, reservists are sent for advanced training in their military specialty. The Army offers almost 500 different skills-training courses, which last an average of fifty-five class days. This constitutes about nine to ten weeks, depending on the amount of weekend leave time.

Obviously, this training period is too short to provide much more than rudimentary instruction, especially in complicated technical fields like engineering or electronics. Reservists, therefore, must plan on continuing their training once they begin serving with their home unit.

Some reservists told me that they had experienced some minor harassment from drill instructors and other personnel because they were "weekend warriors" rather than regular troops. Basically, however, they felt they were treated pretty much the same as the regular troops.

Once a reservist successfully completes both basic and advanced-skills training, he returns to his home community. For the duration of his enlistment, he is required to attend one weekend drill each month and one fifteen-day training period each year.

Reservists receive four days' pay for each training weekend. For attendance purposes, the weekends are divided into four training sessions. If a reservist is absent without excuse from any part of a weekend, he will be required to make up the time. Anyone who misses nine or more training sessions a year without permission will be processed for discharge as a "nonparticipant." In the Air Force, if someone has four unexcused absences (one training weekend) in a year, it will not be credited as a "good" year for purposes of computing retirement eligibility.

In recent years, the reserves have become much more flexible in their scheduling of the required two-week training period. It used to be that everyone in a reserve unit attended training camp during the same two weeks, usually in July or August. Now, reserve units rotate their members' two-week commitments over the entire year.

One Michigan Air Guard unit may be typical of this trend. Virtually all of its members were sent, individually or in small groups, to train with Air Force units in ten other states and in three foreign countries during 1988. Across the board, reservists are much more likely to train with foreign-based units today.

More than 47,000 Army reservists trained abroad as part of the Overseas Deployment Training Program in 1987. Many Army units, however, still continue their tradition of traveling as a group to summer camp for training.

Reserve units also have begun to contract out some of their skills training to local community colleges and vocational schools. They are doing this to save money and also because it spares reservists from having to travel long distances for training.

The number of uniformed reservists who work full-time for the Guard and Reserves has more than doubled in recent years. The military has been replacing civilian employees with reservists who are called "military technicians." Today, there are 173,000 technicians performing a wide range of administrative and technical jobs. These workers are not subject to the Uniform Code of Military Justice during their normal workweek. They are, however, considered to be on active duty during their weekend drills and two-week training periods, just like other reservists.

In recent decades, the distinctions between Reserve and Guard have lessened. Today, they operate under similar federal rules and regulations. As mentioned earlier, Guard units are normally under the control of the individual state governors. A few years ago, a number of state governors began withholding permission for their Guard units to be sent for training and combat exercises in Central America, particularly in Honduras. They were opposed to the Reagan Administration using their Guard units as a way of getting around Congressional opposition to using active-duty GI's in the region. They also feared "another Vietnam" if Reagan continued to use the U.S. military to help the Contras overthrow the Nicaraguan government.

The Pentagon pushed a law through Congress that stripped the governors of any authority over where their Guard units could be sent for training. Several governors joined a lawsuit challenging this law as unconstitutional. In 1989, a federal appeals court rejected this challenge, ruling that the Pentagon can send Guard units wherever it likes.

RESERVE LIFE TODAY

Training Hazards

As noted earlier, Pentagon policy today is to send reservists to train with active-duty troops whenever possible. This emphasis on "realistic" training tends to increase the risk of injury and accidental death. For instance, six members of the Delaware National Guard were killed when their military helicopter crashed during training at Camp Edwards, MA., in June 1989. A month later, two members of Nebraska's National Guard lost their lives when an armored personnel carrier rolled on top of them during a training exercise at Fort Carson, CO., in which 12,000 reservists participated.

Some of these accidents are probably caused by the reservists' inexperience with military equipment. For example, news reports of the Delaware Guard tragedy reported that their chopper crashed only 2,500 feet from a civilian airport while trying to land in "dense, low-lying fog."

This trend toward "realistic" training will probably continue since reservists are slated for immediate deployment in the Pentagon's future war planning.

Restrictions on Liability

As with active-duty GI's, the spouses and children of reservists killed in training "accidents" are barred from suing the federal government for negligence. Survivors must be content with whatever insurance or survivors' benefits are paid by the Department of Veterans' Affairs. Injured reservists are likewise barred from suing.

Incidentally, reservists who receive medical or dental treatment at military health facilities also are barred from suing if they suffer injury or death due to medical malpractice. The U.S. Supreme Court once again endorsed this doctrine of immunity in June 1989 by upholding a lower court's ruling that a Marine widow could not sue for her husband's death following the extraction of a wisdom tooth by military dentists. The Court has cited "national security" as one reason for the rule, even though this case involved only routine dental care under peacetime conditions.

Criminal Justice

Members of the Reserves are covered by the Uniform Code of Military Justice (UCMJ), the military's strict criminal code, whenever they are on training status. As explained in Chapter 5, the military punishes many types of conduct, such as disrespect to an officer, that would not be crimes in civilian society. Reservists who spend relatively little time on active-training status must be careful not to confuse civilian standards of conduct with those of the military.

A few years ago, a Navy reservist named Caputo was caught with a large amount of LSD during his two-week training hitch. For some reason, the Navy failed to bring criminal charges before his training ended. When Caputo reported for his regular weekend drill, he was arrested. A military appeals court reversed Caputo's conviction for drug possession, declaring that the Navy lost criminal jurisdiction over the reservist once he was released from the two-week training session. Since his weekend training was not considered active-duty service, he could not be court-martialed during this period.

This ruling angered many in Congress and the Pentagon. As a result, the law regarding criminal jurisdiction was changed. Now, all types of Reserve training are covered by the UCMJ. National Guard members continue to be governed by criminal codes that have been adopted by individual state legislatures, unless they are on "federal status." The state codes tend to be quite similar to the UCMJ, although there may be variations from state to state. Normally, Guard members will be on "state status" during training periods unless they leave U.S. territory. Then they will automatically be transferred to "federal status" for the duration of their foreign training. Guard members are also considered to be on "federal status" while they undergo basic and advanced skills training.

Congress also changed the law so that reservists now can be ordered back to active-duty status solely for the purpose of trying them for alleged crimes or administering nonjudicial punishment (Article 15's).

Homosexuality

For the last decade, the U.S. military has had a policy of discharging anyone whom the command believes has engaged in homosexual acts or "is likely to engage in them." Thousands of service members have had their military careers terminated simply because of their sexual orientation. Each of the military service branches, including the Guard and Reserves, has regulations that state that homosexuality is "incompatible with military service" and that it "seriously impairs the accomplishment of the military mission."

In addition, some GI's and reservists are court-martialed for sexual crimes if military prosecutors have evidence of homosexual conduct. Lengthy prison sentences as well as "bad" discharges commonly follow conviction.

Reservists may (mistakenly) assume that since they spend so little time on active duty, their units will not be concerned about their sexual orientation. In fact, many reservists have been involuntarily discharged as homosexuals in recent years.

Two recent cases in which homosexual reservists fought the military's practice of discharge or denial of reenlistment have received extensive publicity. The case of Lt. Ellen Nesbitt of Albany, NY, was mentioned in Chapter 7. She was involuntarily discharged after nine years in her Air National Guard unit and a promotion to officer. A routine background check for a security clearance revealed that she was homosexual.

Sgt. Miriam Ben-Shalom also had served honorably for many years with an Army Reserve unit in Milwaukee, WI. After she had become a public advocate for gay rights in her community, Ben-Shalom was denied the right to reenlist. After a legal battle that extended over several years, a federal appeals court in Chicago finally ruled in August 1989 that the Army Reserves could refuse her reenlistment solely because of her sexual orientation. The Supreme Court later refused to review this decision.

Activation to Military Duty

Under current law, the president can order as many as 200,000 members of the National Guard or Reserves to active duty for up to ninety days by simply signing an Executive Order. He can take such action without seeking the approval of Congress. When President Truman activated reservists during the Korean War and President Kennedy did the same during the Berlin crisis in 1961, it evoked a storm of protest and caused serious domestic political problems.

Individual reservists, however, can be placed on active duty for failing to attend training sessions or otherwise failing to meet their commitments. Both the Guard and Reserves have regulations that allow such involuntary activation. In practice, however, such action is no longer common. A spokesperson for the Air National Guard stated that individuals who miss more than nine training sessions a year (slightly more than two weekend drills) are routinely discharged, rather than placed on active duty. They usually receive an honorable discharge, but are barred from reenlisting.

Drug Interdiction Programs

Recently, Congress amended the law to increase the military's participation in law-enforcement operations against drug smuggling. In 1988, Army and Air National Guard units in twenty-nine states participated in a total of 370 anti-drug "missions." Reserve units, particularly from the southern-border states, are expected to play an increasingly active role in such operations in the future. So far, there have been no known casualties among reservists, but there are obvious risks when reservists become involved in attempting to interdict and capture armed and ruthless drug couriers.

Chapter 9

Getting Out/Veterans' Rights

As I explained earlier, the military is a distinct subculture with its own rules and customs. There will always be some who join in good faith, not realizing that they will find military life intolerable.

Other GI's adapt easily to military life but are forced to seek early discharge because of illness or family misfortune. Finally, there are those who discover that participating in an institution that exists to wage war and kill people is morally repugnant to them.

In general, the military expects its members to serve their full term of enlistment before being discharged. If a GI becomes physically or mentally disabled, obtaining a discharge can be fairly routine. But in many other instances, even where the facts support a compassionate discharge, GI's find it difficult to win early release.

Years ago, sergeants commonly dismissed GI concerns about their families with a stock phrase: "If the Army had wanted you to have a wife, it would have issued you one." Although military commanders today are more sensitive to the personal problems of GI's than in the past, there is still an ingrained attitude that a GI shouldn't allow his family problems to interfere with his job.

The rules and procedures governing early discharge are quite complicated and vary from one service to another. They can best be explained by dividing military service into three distinct phases: the period of enrollment in the delayed-entry program, the first six months (180 days) of active duty, and active duty after 180 days. The rules for obtaining an early discharge are different for each period. Each is discussed separately.

THE DELAYED-ENTRY PROGRAM (DEP)

This program was discussed in Chapter 1. The vast majority of military recruits spend time in the DEP before they report for active duty. When enlisting, they promise to report for active duty on a specific date up to a year later.

The DEP serves three valuable functions for the military. First, it allows the Pentagon's manpower planners to control the entry of new personnel so that they can be matched to job slots as they become available. For instance, if the Army knows that it will need fifty tank drivers eight months from now, it can assign DEP dates so that replacements will be trained and ready when the openings occur.

Second, the DEP allows GI's to stay in their home communities for a few months after they enlist. They then can help recruiters sign up their friends and classmates. Each of the services has a system of rewards for those who help in this way, including excelerated promotion when they complete basic training.

Third, the interval between enlisting and actually going into the military helps cushion the recruit from the immediate effects of his decision. Recruiters often reassure high school graduates that they will be able to enjoy their "senior summer" with their classmates before shipping out. It's a little like department stores that sell Christmas gifts by promising that no payments will be due until the following year.

From the military's point of view, however, there are certain risks involved in allowing several months to pass before recruits are required to report. Currently, about one in ten recruits fails to "ship" on the assigned reporting date. To keep this attrition rate from going even higher, all recruiters are required to stay in close contact with enlistees "in the DEP," as it is called. Recruits are commonly told that they must check in every two weeks. Sometimes they also are told to attend DEP meetings at the recruiting station.

Your Legal Rights While in the DEP

On your first visit to the MEPS, you were physically and mentally evaluated. When the processing was completed, you signed a "Confirmation of Enlistment" and swore an oath of allegiance. These two acts placed you in the Inactive Reserves for the duration of the delayed-entry period (up to 365 days). You are *not*, however, on active duty, and you are not subject to the UCMJ. Therefore, you do not have to obey recruiters who order you to attend so-called DEP meetings or to perform filing, phoning, or other tasks at the recruiting office. Military regulations strictly forbid DEP recruits from engaging in any of the following: marching or drilling, organized calisthenics or endurance runs, firing weapons, overnight hikes, camping trips, or similar outings.

You should be aware, however, that recruiters often reward those who *do* attend DEP meetings and display a "cooperative" attitude with special certificates and supportive letters to the drill sergeants at basic.

My impression is that recruiters often misrepresent the nature of the DEP commitment, relying on the ignorance of most recruits. They use two different approaches with recruits who express doubts about reporting for active duty. One is to remind them of the opportunities offered by the military. They may add appeals to patriotism, keeping one's word, and "standing tall" as a man. If this fails, they will resort to threats of what happens to those who do not report (arrest, jail, and public disgrace).

Although the recruiter will tell you it is impossible to get out of your DEP contract, it is actually done every day. Some recruiters have told enlistees that they must wait until basic training (when it's too late) to request separation. The military's regulations provide a number of grounds for winning release before having to go to active duty. In addition, spokespeople for the Army and Air Force told me that anyone with a DEP contract who did not want to report would be released from their commitment (see Chapter 1). Such statements of "official policy," however, do not excuse you from following the military's procedures for seeking discharge.

If you are having serious doubts about your decision to join the military, the best time to seek separation is *now*, when you are still in the DEP. Once you go on active duty, it becomes much more difficult to obtain a discharge. This is not to say that winning separation during the DEP period is easy, because it isn't. But it is a lot less stressful than fighting for release once you are in uniform and subject to military discipline.

A Word of Advice

If you want to get out of your enlistment contract, you should arrange to have an attorney or a civilian counselor help prepare your request (see Appendix for referrals). If you have low-income status, you may be eligible for free representation by a Legal Aid or Legal Services lawyer. You need outside help for two reasons. One, the rules are complicated and an experienced counselor can help you assemble the strongest case for discharge. Two, the military may treat your request differently if an outside lawyer or counselor is involved.

Once the recruiters learn that you don't want to go on active duty, they will try to get you to change your mind. (A recruiter's quota is affected when an enlistee fails to report.) In one recent case in New York City, a Puerto Rican man who applied for release from a DEP contract was summoned to the recruiting command several times. On his final visit, a Hispanic recruiter pleaded with him not to "dishonor" Puerto Ricans by refusing to serve.

Your counselor can help you stand up to any pressure recruiters may apply. At the outset, you should have your counselor or lawyer send a letter to the commander of recruiters, stating that "under no circumstances" will you report for active duty, and that "no manner of counseling" will cause you to change your mind. If a recruiter calls you or tries to visit your home, you do not have to talk with him. Tell him to contact your legal representative if he wants to discuss your application for discharge. However, you may have to agree to an interview to present your reasons for discharge so that recruiting personnel can evaluate your sincerity and credibility.

Grounds for Separation from the DEP

Military regulations provide a number of reasons for separation. These regulations change from time to time and vary from one branch to another. The following summaries are intended only as an introduction to the subject. Be sure to check the current regulation before preparing your application for release.

Applicants can base their petition on more than one category for separation. It is best, however, to concentrate on one or two strong ones, rather than throwing in marginal claims. Categories that are starred (*) also can be used by those on active duty as a basis for discharge, although the criteria may be different.

- *Acceptance to college or vocational school.* This is one of the most common reasons why people in the DEP want out of the military. Sometimes young people give in to a persistent recruiter before really checking out college or other job-training opportunities. You must furnish proof of acceptance from the college or vocational program you plan to attend. It helps if the school has awarded you a scholarship or tuition aid, although it is not essential. Because recruiters work closely with high school educators, the military doesn't like to appear to be interfering with a young person's quest for education.

- *Hardship.** To qualify for a hardship release, a member of the recruit's immediate family (spouse, parent, sibling, or child) must suffer from a serious and long-term physical or mental condition that began (or substantially worsened) after the recruit enlisted. In other words, if your mother or daughter had a serious health problem at the time you joined up, the military will not allow you to base a discharge request on this condition. Also, if there is any way that the hardship can be alleviated without releasing the GI, his request will be denied. Requests for hardship discharge are scrutinized very closely, both in the DEP and on active duty. In general, it is quite difficult to obtain release for this reason.

- *Pregnancy.* The military will not allow an expectant mother to go on active duty. Each female recruit is also given a pregnancy test during basic training. Those with "positive" results are discharged, although sometimes they are allowed to enlist at a later date.

- *Underage.** No one younger than seventeen years can enlist legally—period. Between seventeen and eighteen years, a youth must secure the written consent of both parents or guardians. If an enrollee falls into either category, it provides the basis for release.

- *Homosexuality.** The military will not enlist anyone who is homosexual. You have a better chance for release on this basis if you realized your sexual orientation only *after* you enlisted. This is because the enlistment contract you signed required you to state that you were not homosexual and that you did not intend to engage in homosexual acts while in the military. If you contradict this in your application for separation, the military could charge you with the crime of fraudulent enlistment.

- *Medical or psychological disability.** The Army has developed a long list of medical and psychological conditions that prevent a person from being enlisted. All the services rely on this index, called the "Procurement Medical Fitness Standards," to evaluate recruits' health problems. If the physical or mental condition you suffer from appears in the index and you can provide independent medical documentation, your chances of being separated are quite good.

- *Marriage.* In some instances, marriage during the DEP period will disqualify a recruit from going on active duty.

- *Conscientious objection (CO).** Most young people have never given much thought to their personal philosophy concerning the use of violence or participating in war. For some, putting on the uniform will force them to consider these issues for the first time. Some people are conscientious objectors, even though they may not realize it until the military's definition is explained to them. Persons who apply for discharge as CO's during the DEP period do not have to go through the complicated application process that is required of those on active duty. The applicant need only submit a statement explaining how his moral, ethical, or religious beliefs have led him to a "firm, fixed, and sincere objection to war in any form or the bearing of arms." Letters from teachers, clergymen, or relatives attesting to the sincerity of the applicant's beliefs should be attached. A short book, *Advice for Conscientious Objectors in the Armed Forces*, published by CCCO is very helpful (see Appendix).

- *Recruiter fraud, erroneous enlistment.* Sometimes enlistees rely on promises made by recruiters that turn out to be erroneous or false. Also, recruiters may enlist people who are ineligible for various reasons. It is possible to win release from the military if these facts are brought to the attention of the recruiting command.

- *Change in the number of dependents.* Each branch of service places limits on the number of legal dependents (spouse, children, or other family members) that a person can have at the time he enlists. If a new dependent exceeds the allowable number, this may provide the basis for separation.

- *Drug abuse, criminal conviction, or pending civil matter.* If a recruit is charged with a crime or convicted of one during the DEP period, he may be separated, either by the military or on his own application. In some instances, a pending case in civil court may also bar someone from going on active duty.

    In recent years, the Pentagon has spent millions upon millions of dollars to regularly test the urine of every single GI for residues from marijuana, cocaine, and other drugs. Tens of thousands of GI's have been involuntarily discharged and, in some cases, prosecuted for drug use based on these test results. If there's one word that is a red flag to the military command today, it is "drugs."

    Given this atmosphere, any DEP enrollee who documents that he is a drug or alcohol abuser or who enters a treatment program for either probably can get out of his enlistment contract.

- *Apathy or personal problem.* The regulations that define this category are quite vague. Your written statement should underscore your apathetic or indifferent attitude about service and how that may pose problems for the military.

- *Failure of high school senior to graduate.* Some military jobs require that GI's possess high school diplomas. Of course, many other jobs don't, so the military has considerable discretion here. The recruiting command also has the option of extending the applicant's reporting date (to a maximum of 365 days after initial enlistment) so that he can return to school and complete his degree requirements.

- *Entering religious training or being ordained as a minister.* You will need documentation from religious leaders or teachers stating that you are enrolled in religious school or that you have entered religious service as an ordained minister.

- *Enlisted into another branch of the service.* If a recruit decides, say, that he would rather be in the Navy than the Army, it is possible for him to win release from his Army contract for this reason.

- *Failure to report/refusal to go on active duty.* This is a catch-all category that the military can use to separate someone who fails to report. Technically, an individual enlistee doesn't use this category to apply for release. It is used by the military once someone has failed to appear on his reporting date.

  The recruiting command sows a lot of confusion about what will happen to someone who doesn't show up. They often tell enlistees that they will be involuntarily placed on active duty, even if they fail to report. The legal authority for doing this is debatable. At any rate, if you don't show, the military will probably take steps to separate you using the "failure to report" category. As I stated earlier, if you don't want to serve, it is much better to fight the military from *outside*, rather than placing yourself on active duty where you are subject to military authority. Plus, once you have put on the uniform and accepted military pay, you may be considered to have waived certain defenses by "constructively enlisting."

The Procedure for Separation from the DEP

Sometimes fear or indecision will cause you to wait almost until it is time to report before you request a separation. If more time is needed to research and prepare an application, you can ask the recruiting commander to extend your reporting date. No one can spend more than 365 days in the DEP, but in most cases, the original DEP period will not be this lengthy. Be aware that once you file for an extension of time, any promises that the military made about job training or assignment may be wiped out.

Once adequate documentation has been gathered to support your separation request, it should be filed with the recruiting command. The chain of command for review varies from branch to branch. Individual recruiters have no authority to act on your request, so you should bypass them.

You should also send a copy of your complete application to your Congressperson. Call his or her office and try to talk with the staff member who handles military casework. Some staff members will be more helpful than others–it just depends. It is not unusual for hundreds of constituents to complain about military-related problems in the course of a year, so don't make unreasonable demands.

If the local command approves your separation request, you will receive written notification of either an entry-level separation, release from a void enlistment, or discharge, depending on the branch of service. If your request is denied, you should ask that the national recruiting command review this decision. Of course, make sure that your Congressional allies are kept informed of this action.

It is not unusual for an enlistee to learn that his request for separation has been denied just a day or two before he is supposed to report. To reiterate, your best strategy may still be not to go on active duty, although you should discuss this with your counselor or lawyer in advance.

If the national recruiting command will not overrule its local officials, you may also have grounds for filing a lawsuit in federal district court to overturn the military's rulings.

DISCHARGE OR SEPARATION DURING THE FIRST 180 DAYS OF SERVICE

The military considers the first 180 days of active duty to be a probationary period, although they don't tell GI's that. Military commanders have broad discretion to get rid of substandard performers. Most GI's who are dropped during this period receive an "uncharacterized entry-level separation." These people used to be given regular discharges (usually either honorable or general), but the Pentagon decided that this practice detracted from the "integrity" of the honorable discharge, so they stopped it. A

GI also must receive written notice of the proposed separation action and is allowed a few days in which to submit a written rebuttal.

In most instances, the GI will be "separated" rather than discharged, although the net effect is about the same. Everyone today enlists for an eight-year term. Once a person completes the active-duty portion of his contract (usually three or four years) and leaves the military, he will serve out the balance of the eight years in either the Active or Inactive Reserves (or a combination of the two). Those who receive "entry-level separations" are placed in the Inactive Reserves for the remainder of their eight years. Persons on this status perform no military duties, but are subject to activation in time of war.

The military will give discharges (rather than separations) to a few categories of GI's. The Army, for example, discharges those who are dropped for homosexuality, defective enlistment, personality disorders, misconduct, and conscientious objection. The other branches have similar rules.

Although these separation actions are often initiated by the command, GI's who want out can begin the process on their own. These procedures are quite technical, and you should work with an experienced counselor or attorney if at all possible.

Grounds for Discharge of Separation During First 180 Days of Service

- *Conscientious objection.* Persons on active duty must submit a detailed questionnaire and undergo interviews by a military psychiatrist, chaplain, and an investigating officer, who then recommends approval or rejection.

- *Hardship or dependency.* See previous DEP discussion.

- *Pregnancy or childbirth.* A mother on active duty can initiate the request for separation. It is not always granted.

- *Parenthood.* GI's with children must maintain detailed child-care plans that their commander approves. Separation requests based on this category are often denied. Parents may even be assigned to foreign duty where children are not allowed to accompany them.

- *Sole surviving child.* The applicant must be the only remaining child in a family in which a father, mother, sister, or brother was killed (or 100 percent disabled) while serving on active duty.

- *Other designated physical or mental conditions.* Each service will separate personnel for certain health conditions, even though they are not considered "disabilities."

- *Convenience of the government.* This is a catch-all provision used occasionally to get rid of GI's whose cases don't fit neatly into any category.

- *Underage.* If a GI doesn't raise the issue of his age within the first ninety days of active duty, he waives his right to object.

- *Defective enlistment agreement.* To be separated under this provision, there must have been a "material misrepresentation by recruiting personnel." The discharge request must be filed within thirty days of discovery of the error.

- *Entry-level performance and conduct.* This section covers a multitude of problems during training, including ineptitude, failure to adapt to the military, and failure to make satisfactory progress.

- *Homosexuality.* See previous DEP discussion.

- *Drug or alcohol abuse/failure to rehabilitate.* Everyone in uniform has his urine periodically checked for drug residue. Someone who smokes pot very occasionally will be sent to drug rehab if he tests "positive." This assumes, of course, that he is not court-martialed for drug use and tossed out of the military. Drug and alcohol abusers in the military are sent to rehabilitation programs. Those who fail to perform in these programs to the satisfaction of the counselors will be separated from the military.

- *Misconduct.* There are four categories of misconduct. (*Note:* If the misbehavior is serious, the GI will likely be tried by court-martial instead.)

    1. Minor disciplinary infractions. (A pattern of repeated misbehavior is sufficient.)

    2. Pattern of misconduct.

    3. Commission of a serious offense.

    4. Conviction by civilian court.

Persons being dropped under these provisions will normally receive an other-than-honorable discharge (OTH). These are issued by an administrative board composed of officers or NCO's. The respondent has the right to present evidence in his defense to this board.

- *Separation in lieu of court-martial.* Sometimes the military will choose to get rid of someone rather than incur the expense and trouble of a court-martial. Normally, they will give the GI an OTH discharge. In this situation, he will not have the right to present evidence to the administrative board.

- *National security.* A GI who is determined to be a threat to national security will be processed for discharge. Such a determination is usually based on intelligence reports or background investigations concerning political affiliations and activities. Although GI's with radical or "left-wing" sympathies are usually the target of these actions, sometimes soldiers who affiliate with ultra-conservative, Ku Klux Klan–type organizations also are dismissed.

A Word of Warning

There are some employers, both public and private, who expect employees who have served in the military to possess honorable discharges. For them, an "entry-level separation" may be a negative mark. If possible, you should explain that you left the military under honorable circumstances before you were eligible for a clean discharge.

DISCHARGE OR SEPARATION AFTER 180 DAYS OF SERVICE

After six months, GI's who leave the military receive one of several different kinds of discharge; honorable, general, other than honorable, bad conduct, and dishonorable. The last two can be given only as part of a court-martial sentence.

There are also some other discharges and separations that are given in special circumstances; medical discharges, discharges for other designated physical and mental conditions (ODPMC—a subcategory of medical discharge), and separation for unsatisfactory performance.

Veterans who receive either honorable or general discharges (over 90 percent of the total) are entitled to the privileges and benefits of a veteran in good standing. To qualify for benefits from the Department of Veterans Affairs (DVA—formerly the Veterans Administration), a veteran must have been discharged or separated under conditions "other than dishonorable." Vets with either honorable or general discharges are eligible for benefits, but all others are evaluated by the DVA on a case-by-case basis. The DVA has its own rules for determining who qualifies, but most vets with OTH, bad conduct, or dishonorable discharges will be barred from VA benefits.

Each service branch maintains a discharge review board that can change ("upgrade") discharges, except those issued by a general court-martial. Veterans have fifteen years from the date of discharge to seek review by these boards. These boards provide relief in only a minority of cases; the current "success" rate is between 10 and 20 percent of cases reviewed. Nevertheless, veterans with "bad paper" should seek review because eligibility for many benefit programs depends on the type of discharge.

Types of Discharges

- *Honorable*. This discharge is self-explanatory.

- *General*. This discharge is given when the military regards a GI's service as "honest and faithful," but where "significant negative aspects of the member's conduct or performance of duty outweigh positive aspects of the member's military record."

- *Other than honorable (OTH)*. This discharge is given by an administrative board of officers and NCO's.

- *Bad conduct*. This discharge can only be given as part of a sentence by a special or general court-martial.

- *Dishonorable*. This discharge can only be given after conviction by a general court-martial.

- *Medical discharge*. This discharge can be given on the command's initiative or upon application by the affected GI. Each service branch publishes medical standards that list disqualifying physical and mental conditions. A discharge will not be granted unless it is determined that the defect prevents the GI from actually performing his military duties. It is essential that the applicant be examined by a civilian doctor who should prepare a detailed report on his condition. This diagnosis is then given to the military physicians when they conduct their examination. A medical board must be convened by the military to examine the condition and documentation of the GI. This board will authorize any discharge or disability determination.

  If a health problem is due to a condition that existed prior to enlistment, the GI may have to file his discharge request within the first few weeks or months of active duty to qualify.

Seeking medical discharge is a complicated process that requires the expert assistance of a counselor or attorney.

- *Other designated physical or mental conditions.* The Defense Department regulation summarizes this category as follows: "physical or mental conditions, not amounting to disability . . . that potentially interfere with assignment to, or performance of duty. . . . Such conditions may include, but aren't limited to, chronic seasickness or airsickness, enuresis (bed-wetting), and personality disorder."

The services have interpreted this regulation as requiring the discharge of GI's with a host of conditions, including sleepwalking, allergies, obesity, dyslexia, motion sickness, and skin conditions, in addition to those listed above.

GI's subject to discharge under this regulation must be counseled by their commanders regarding their deficiencies and be given an opportunity to correct them, when that is feasible.

- *Separation for unsatisfactory performance.* Military commanders have broad authority to evaluate the performance of a GI as well as his potential. They are empowered to dismiss any GI whose performance they decide is "unsatisfactory." In some cases, GI's who want out have used this regulation successfully. The assistance of an experienced counselor in preparing your request is invaluable.

YOUR RIGHTS AS A VETERAN

There are about 33 million military veterans in the United States today. Long ago, Congress created an agency specifically to provide services to this vast population. The Veterans Administration, which was recently renamed the Department of Veterans Affairs (DVA), grew rapidly after World War II to become the third largest federal agency (after the Pentagon and the Department of Health and Human Services). Today, the DVA has 250,000 employees and an annual budget of nearly $30 billion. It operates the world's largest health system, with 172 hospitals and many additional clinics, hospices, and rest homes.

As a veteran, you may be eligible to participate in a variety of DVA programs. There is only room here to briefly summarize some of the more important ones. You may want to contact veterans' organizations in your community or do more reading on this vast subject (see Bibliography).

As mentioned earlier, the type of military discharge you receive may affect your eligibility for DVA benefits. A vet with an other-than-honorable, bad conduct, or dishonorable discharge usually will not be eligible for benefits. There are exceptions; vets with other than honorables, for example, will usually be given medical care by the DVA. However, as a general rule, vets with "bad paper" should try to win an "upgrade" from a discharge review board.

HEALTH CARE AND MEDICAL TREATMENT

All veterans are theoretically entitled to free medical care at a DVA facility, whether or not their health problems are related to military service. In reality, vets whose health problems are not "service connected" may find that obtaining treatment is difficult.

Today, the DVA's medical system suffers from some of the same systemic problems as the military's system. Its medical facilities and staffing levels have not been expanded to keep pace with the ever-growing number of patients. In fact, some DVA hospitals have had to reduce existing services because of budgetary problems.

Many veterans complain that they must wait for hours to be treated by rude and often incompetent medical staff. Others are bothered by a "revolving door" treatment system in which the patient never sees the same doctor twice. The system's heavy reliance on medical students and foreign medical graduates is another common complaint. Like the military, the DVA has had difficulty hiring and retaining physicians because the salary structure is not competitive with what doctors can earn in private practice.

The DVA's medical system, which treats several million patients each year, is a vast bureaucracy that cannot provide the kind of individualized care offered by some private practitioners. On the other hand, there are many dedicated health professionals in the system who can provide patients with the latest medical technology, all at no charge.

Anyone considering becoming a DVA patient should weigh the risks posed by overcrowding, lax peer pressure among doctors at some hospitals, and the risks posed by the limits placed on recovery for medical malpractice. Injured patients (or their survivors) must use the Federal Tort Claims Act to sue, and this places a number of restrictions on liability. Not only is there no provision for trial by jury, but punitive damages are also prohibited, no matter how reckless or grossly negligent the medical staff may have been. Assuming that a veteran has medical insurance allowing him the choice, he can probably expect better care from private health-care providers than at a DVA hospital.

Access to DVA Medical Care

There are complicated rules and regulations that govern the order in which patients are admitted and treated at a DVA hospital.

Generally speaking, to receive treatment today, a veteran must have one of the following:

- A "service-connected" disability (the injury occurred or worsened while the veteran was on active duty).

- A disability for which the veteran was discharged from the military, although not "service connected."

- An award of disability by the DVA.

- Exposure to "Agent Orange" (herbicide used by U.S. military in Vietnam) or radioactive fallout during U.S. atomic bomb tests, while on active duty.

- Sixty-five years or older and disabled (although not "service connected").

Admission to a DVA hospital for treatment is granted in the following order:

1. Emergencies where serious injury or death could occur.

2. Readmission of patients currently receiving DVA treatment.

3. Treatment of vets with "service-connected" disabilities.

4. Active-duty personnel who are retiring from the service.

5. Vets who need treatment to begin or continue vocational rehabilitation.

6. Vets for whom DVA officials have requested medical evaluation.

7. Vets who receive DVA benefits and are patients at non-DVA hospitals.

8. Some vets who request transfer from another DVA hospital or who are being treated as outpatients at another DVA facility.

Whether or not you will be admitted for treatment depends on the patient load at the hospital to which you apply. Some DVA facilities are chronically overbooked, especially in large cities, while others will accommodate patients in most or all of the above categories.

In addition to hospital care, the DVA also provides a broad range of outpatient medical services to veterans. Sometimes the DVA will reimburse veterans for treatment by private doctors when their system becomes overloaded.

OTHER BENEFIT PROGRAMS

The rules and regulations that govern eligibility for the various assistance programs for veterans are extremely complex, and what appears below is only the barest of outlines. Each of the national veterans organizations (the American Legion, Disabled American Veterans, etc.) maintains a network of claims representatives who can assist you with filing a claim. After the Civil War, Congress passed a law making it a crime for a lawyer to receive more than $10 for helping a veteran fight his claim. The law's original purpose was to protect vets and their widows from dishonest lawyers, but its long-term effect has been to undermine veterans' ability to win complicated compensation cases. There have been efforts to overturn this law, both in the courts and in Congress, but to date, it is still on the books.

DISABILITY COMPENSATION

This is one of the DVA's largest programs. In 1987, it paid $10.5 billion to two-and-a-half million veterans with "service-connected" disabilities. These payments are made irrespective of a veteran's income.

If you have a health problem that you believe was caused (or made worse) by your service in the military, you can apply to have it recognized as "service connected" by the DVA. This is a two-stage process. First, you must establish that your health problem developed (or was worsened) during military duty, and second, that the problem has disabled you to a measurable degree.

Your claim for disability will be reviewed by a Rating Board. These boards have three members: a medical doctor and two civil servants who specialize in evaluating such claims. There is at least one Rating Board in each of the DVA's fifty-two regional offices.

These boards rely on a rating schedule that currently lists about 720 different medical conditions (diagnostic codes), which are arranged by body system; for example, gynecological or cardiovascular. They apply medical criteria to determine the severity of the alleged condition. If they find disability, they assign a precise degree (10 percent, 20 percent, and so on) that determines the amount the veteran will be paid. Sometimes they find "service connection" but vote a disability award of zero. Incidentally, the armed forces use the same rating schedule to evaluate the claims of active-duty GI's for disability.

In 1987–88, the Government Accounting Office (GAO) conducted an in-depth investigation of these boards. It found that the rating schedule contained such obsolete medical criteria that it made it "almost impossible" for the DVA to operate a uniform and equitable claims system. It described many of the criteria as "incomplete and outdated," noting that data for ten out of fourteen body systems had not been revised since 1978, at the latest.

The GAO report urged the DVA to conduct a comprehensive review of all these criteria and to install a system to ensure that the data is kept up to date in the future. The DVA Administrator agreed to implement both recommendations, although he argued that despite the changes, the benefits awarded to veterans would not vary much.

The credibility of the DVA's disability process suffered another blow in 1989 when a federal judge in San Francisco threw out regulations that the DVA had been using since 1984 to deny veterans' disability claims for Agent Orange injuries. Agent Orange, a toxic herbicide, was used extensively by the U.S. military during the Vietnam War to deny food and cover to the Viet Cong.

In 1984, Congress passed legislation to force the DVA to look more compassionately on the claims of veterans for health problems related to Agent Orange. Until then, the DVA had adamantly refused to acknowledge any connection between the spray and veterans' declining health. Despite the law, the agency continued to require that claimants prove a causal link between their illness and Agent Orange, something that none could do. Congress had adopted a less stringent standard, that showing "significant statistical association" was enough. As a result of the DVA's practices, only *five* veterans, out of 33,272 who filed, were successful in winning compensation.

The federal judge ordered the DVA to overhaul its regulations on Agent Orange claims so that they conform with the 1984 law. Surprisingly, a few days later, the Administrator announced that the DVA would abide by the ruling and not appeal the ruling to a higher court. It is unclear at present just how many of the 33,272 veterans who filed disability claims will now receive favorable action.

A Word of Advice

It is important that you file your disability claim as soon after you leave the military as possible. If you file within a year of discharge and later win disability, you will be paid for that entire year. If you wait more than a year to file, you will be paid only from the date disability was awarded.

Congress has adopted laws stating that forty different chronic diseases and fifteen tropical ones will be "presumed" to be service connected if they appear within a certain period of time *after* the veteran leaves active duty (the time period varies with each disease). With these, the only issue for the DVA to decide is the degree of disability (if any) suffered by the claimant.

You will need to acquire copies of all your military records, including, of course, your medical treatment history. In addition to this, you will need to develop independent medical evidence, including examinations conducted by your own physician(s).

Appeal of a Denied Disability Claim

If your claim is denied outright or if you are awarded a lower percentage than you feel is justified, you may want to appeal. Again, because the rules by which the DVA hears appeals are complicated and change frequently, you will need to work with an experienced claims representative.

Your first step will be to file a Notice of Disagreement at the same DVA office that denied your claim. You must do this within one year of the date of the negative ruling. In response, the agency will prepare a Statement of the Case, summarizing the evidence the board relied on, as well as the rules and regulations that it applied in reaching its decision.

Depending on the nature of your claim, you may want to exercise your right to have your claim reconsidered by a different Rating Board. You have the right to appear personally before this second panel, along with your claims representative, and to present evidence. In most cases, the second board will endorse the ruling of its predecessor.

If you are unhappy with how this second review turns out, you may appeal your case to the Board of Veterans Appeal (BVA) in Washington, D.C. The BVA is composed of sixty-five members (all DVA employees) who review local decisions from across the country, in panels of three. Currently, the BVA acts favorably in about one in eight cases presented to it, although it sometimes sends other cases back to the local Regional Offices for further consideration.

It used to be that a negative decision by the BVA was the end of the road, with few exceptions. In 1986, however, Congress changed this by creating a new federal court specifically to review certain decisions by the BVA. For the first time, veterans who wish to appeal their cases to this court may hire lawyers and pay them reasonable fees.

In addition, veterans have always had a limited right to sue in federal court where the actions of the DVA were alleged to be unconstitutional or clearly against the law.

PENSIONS

Veterans who fall within certain income guidelines and are rated as disabled may qualify for a pension from the DVA. In fiscal 1987, 1.3 million veterans (or their survivors) were paid a total of $3.8 billion in pension benefits. The maximum monthly payment for a 100 percent disabled veteran without dependents was $518.

For our purposes, there are two basic pensions: the Improved Pension and the Improved Death Pension. The requirements for receiving each are listed on pages 209-210.

Improved Pension (veteran must meet all conditions)

1. Service during "war time"; for example, Korean or Vietnam War. Actual duty in a war zone is not required.

2. "Permanently disabled" (a condition that continues throughout life).

3. "Totally disabled" (a sliding scale based on age; at sixty-five you are presumed totally disabled).

4. Must fall within income guidelines.

5. Must have discharge reflecting "other than dishonorable service."

Under the improved pension program, a veteran with a wife and one dependent child received $8,709 in 1985.

Improved Death Pension (veteran must meet all conditions)

1. Payable only to widow or dependent child of deceased vet.

2. "War time" service required (same as above).

3. Veteran's death cannot have been caused by military duty.

4. Veteran's discharge reflects "other than dishonorable service."

Under the improved death pension program, a widow loses her pension if she remarries. A child who remains enrolled in school is eligible until twenty-three years old. A widow with one child received $5,167 in 1985.

Death Benefits

Widows, children, or dependent parents may be eligible for benefits upon the death of a veteran. There are separate forms and procedures for this category of benefits.

OTHER BENEFIT PROGRAMS

The DVA also operates a number of other programs that benefit veterans, including:

- Loan guarantees for the purchase of a house or trailer.
- Life insurance.
- Small Business Loans (administered by the Small Business Administration).

In addition, all states operate a variety of benefit and assistance programs for veterans. These include:

- One-time bonus payments (especially for Vietnam-era vets).
- Home and farm loans.
- Hiring preference for state and local government jobs.
- Tax exemptions.
- State-operated "old age homes" for vets.
- Tuition waivers or reductions.

Selective Bibliography

Books

Army Times Staff. *Handbook for Military Families, 1989 Edition.* Springfield, VA: Army Times Publishing, 1989.

Baker, Mark. *NAM* (combatants' accounts). New York: William Morrow, 1981.

Berryman, Sue. *Who Serves?* Boulder, CO: Westview Press, 1988.

Binkin, Martin and Kaufmann, Wm. *US Army Guard & Reserve: Rhetoric, Realities, Risk.* Washington, D.C.: Brookings Institution, 1989.

Binkin, Martin and Eitelberg, Mark, et al. *Blacks and the Military.* Washington, D.C.: Brookings Institution, 1982.

Bonior, Champlin and Kolly. *The Vietnam Vet: A History of Neglect.* Westport, CT: Praeger Publishers, 1984.

Bowman, W. Little, R., and Sicilia, G.T., eds. *The All Volunteer Force After a Decade.* Elmsford, NY: Pergamon-Brassey, 1986.

Campbell, Duncan. *The Unsinkable Aircraft Carrier: American Military Power in Britain.* London: Paladin Books, 1986.

Coates, James and Kilian, James. *Heavy Losses: The Dangerous Decline of American Defense.* New York: Viking, 1985.

Crocker, Lawrence, Lt. Col. *The Army Officer's Guide, 44th Ed.* Harrisburg, PA: Stackpole, 1988.

Fallows, James. *National Defense.* New York: Vintage, 1981.

Fussell, Paul. *Wartime: Understanding and Behavior in the Second World War.* New York: Oxford, 1989.

Gabriel, Richard. *Military Incompetence.* New York: Hill & Wang, 1985.

Gabriel, Richard and Savage, Paul. *Crisis in Command: Mismanagement in the Army.* New York: Hill & Wang, 1978.

Halberstadt, Hans. *N.T.C.: A Primer of Modern Land Combat*. Novato, CA: Presidio Press, 1989.

Halloran, Richard. *To Arm a Nation*. New York: Macmillan, 1986.

Holm, Jeanne, Brig. General. *Women in the Military*. Novato, CA: Presidio Press, 1982.

Kaplan, Fred. *The Wizards of Armageddon*. New York: Simon & Schuster, 1983.

Kubey, C., Addelestone, D., et al. *The Viet Vet Survival Guide*, New York: Ballantine, 1985.

Langone, John. *AIDS, The Facts*. Boston: Little, Brown, 1988.

Luttwak, Edward. *The Pentagon and the Art of War*. New York: Touchstone, 1985.

Myers, James and Scott, Elizabeth. *Getting Skilled, Getting Ahead*. Princeton, NJ: Peterson's Guides, 1989.

Nalty, Bernard C. *Strength for the Fight: A History of Black Americans in the Military*. New York: Free Press, 1986.

Palmer, General Bruce. *The 25 Year War: America's Military Role in Vietnam*. New York: Touchstone, 1985.

Powers, Helen. *Parent's Guide to the Five U.S. Service Academies*. Harrisburg, PA: Stackpole, 1986.

Radine, Lawrence. *The Taming of the Troops*. Westport, CT: Greenwood Press, 1977.

Rivkin, R. & Stichman, B. *The Rights of Military Personnel*. New York: Avon/Discus, 1977.

Roberts, Ralph. *The Veteran's Guide to Benefits*. New York: Signet, 1989.

Saywell, Shelley. *Women in War*. New York: Viking, 1985.

Schneider, Dorothy and Carl J. *Sound Off!: American Military Women Speak Out*. New York: E.P. Dutton, 1988.

Scowcroft, Brent, ed. *Military Service in the U.S.* New York: Prentice-Hall, 1982.

Segal, David R. *Recruiting for Uncle Sam*. Lawrence KS: University Press of KS, 1988.

Skinner, Michael. *USN: Naval Operations in the '80s*. Novato, CA: Presidio Press, 1986.

Uhl, Michael and Ensign, Tod. *GI Guinea Pigs*. New York: Playboy Press, 1980.

West, Luther C., Lt. Col. *They Call It Justice.* New York: Viking Press, 1977.

Wilson, George. *Supercarrier.* New York: Scribner's, 1986.

Wilson, George. *Mud Soldiers: Life Inside the New American Army.* New York: Scribner's, 1989.

Reports and Pamphlets

General Accounting Office. *Military Jury System Needs Safeguards Found in Civilian Federal Courts.* 1977. Report FPCD 76–48.

General Accounting Office. *Navy Training: Safety Has Been Improved, But More Still Needs to Be Done.* 1989. Report NSIAD 89–119.

Greenpeace and Institute for Policy Studies, *Naval Accidents, 1945-1988.* 1989, Washington, D.C.

Reserve Forces Policy Board. *Reserve Component Programs, Annual Report—Fiscal 1988.* Washington, D.C.: Office of the Secretary of Defense.

Appendix

Legal Referrals and Military Counseling Organizations

Citizen Soldier
Tricia Critchfield
175 Fifth Avenue, Suite 808
New York, NY 10010
(212) 777-3470

American Friends Service Committee
821 Euclid Avenue
Syracuse, NY 13210
(315) 475-4822

Central Committee for Conscientious Objectors (CCCO)
2208 South Street
Philadelphia, PA 19146
(215) 454-4626

American Friends Service Committee
Harold Jordan
1501 Cherry Street
Philadelphia, PA 19102
(215) 241-7176

National Interreligious Service Board for Conscientious Objectors (NISBCO)
1601 Connecticut Avenue N.W., Suite 750
Washington, DC 20009
(202) 483-4510

Atlanta Peace Alliance
Brian Taylor
P.O. Box 54225
Atlanta, GA 30308
(404) 378-5551

Concerned Americans for Military Improvement (CAMI)
Joe and Joan Connors
P.O. Box 6226
Ocala, FL 32678
(904) 368-7608

Veterans Education Project
Tom Fischer
P.O. Box 431
Tallahassee, FL 32302
(904) 222-5845

Instituto Puertorriqueno de Derechos
Civiles
Adalina De Jesus Morales
Calle Julian Blanco #11
Rio Piedras, PR 00925
(809) 754-7390

Midwest Committee for Military Counseling (MCMC)
Ray Parrish
343 S. Dearborn Street, Suite 1113
Chicago, IL 60604
(312) 939-3349

National Lawyers Guild Military Task Force
Kathy Gilberd
1168 Union, Suite 201
San Diego, CA 92101
(619) 233-1701

Central Committee for Conscientious Objectors (CCCO–Western Region)
P.O. Box 42249
San Francisco, CA 94142
(415) 752-7766

Northwest Military and Draft Counseling
John Grueschow
1422 SE Tacoma
Portland, OR
(503) 238-0605

Seattle Draft and Military Counseling Center
225 N. 70th Street
Seattle, WA 98103
(206) 789-2751

Bill Boston
Military Counseling Network
c/o Jugendhaus Sindelfingen-Mitte
7024 Sindelfingen
West Germany
07031/87104 or 0711-625109

Glossary of Military Terms

AIT: Advanced individual training (in MOS) (training for a specific job)
APR: Airman's Performance Report
Article 15: Disciplinary action, as provided by regulation
ASVAB: Armed Services Vocational Aptitude Battery
AWOL: Absent without (official) leave
BTZ (below the zone): Basis for early promotion; deep selection
boot camp: Basic training in the seagoing services
bootstrap program: One of several programs by which the military prepares
    enlisted members for officer candidacy, usually by paying for their
    educations
BX: Base exchange, store
cammies: Camouflage uniforms
chain of command: Hierarchy of authority. To register complaints or seek
    help, the servicemember must work first through his or her own supervi-
    sor, then step by step to the next highest authority.
chaptered out: Involuntarily separated by regulation
CNO: Chief of Naval Operations
CO: Commanding officer
commissioned officer: An officer whose rank and power in active service is
    conferred by the President; ranks as second lieutenant or higher in the
    Army, Air Force, or Marine Corps, or as ensign or higher in the Navy or
    Coast Guard.
CONUS: Within the continental United States
counseling statement: Written reprimand
CQ: Charge of Quarters; responsibility for the order and safety of a barracks,
    office, and so on
cut-off score: Number of points required for promotion within a particular
    MOS
DACOWITS: Defense Advisory Committee on Women in the Services
deep selection: Basis for early promotion
detailer: Person who assigns servicemembers to particular positions and
    places
DI: Drill instructor
Dining In; Dining Out: Party for officers only; party for officers and their
    guests
DO: Deck Officer
DOD: Department of Defense
EO: Equal Opportunity Office, whose function is to protect the civil rights of
    minorities
first sergeant; first shirt: Senior NCO in charge of personnel problems.
GS rate: General Services (civil service) rank
gunny: Gunnery sergeant, Marine Corps
Human Relations Council: Group designated to work out equal opportunity
    and similar problems
IG: Inspector General
Joint Domicile, Joint Household, Joint Spouse: Programs designed to assign
    military wife and military husband together
LDO: Limited duty officer, who functions within a single field of interest
lines: Ropes (seagoing services)
LORAN: Long-range navigation
MAC: Military Airlift Command

mast: A hearing, in the seagoing services. A *captain's mast* is a hearing before the captain; a *request mast* is by the request of the servicemember.

master-at-arms: Military police for Navy and Coast Guard

max: Attain a score established as the maximum, especially on a physical fitness test

medevac: Evacuation for medical reasons

meritorious promotion: Promotion before expected time, or without usual tests

MK: Mechanic MOS

monitor: Person who assigns servicemembers to particular positions and places; detailer

MOS: Military occupational specialty; a numerical code, for example, 76-Whiskey (petroleum specialist), 11-Bravo or 11-Bang-bang (infantryman)

MP: Military police

NBC: Nuclear/biological/chemical defense

NCO, noncom: Noncommissioned officer (in enlisted ranks)

NCOIC: Noncommissioned officer in charge at a given time and place

OCS: Officer Candidate School

OER: Officer Evaluation Report

OIC: Officer in charge at a given time and place

on profile: Restricted in physical activities

OTS: Officer Training School

OUTUS: Outside the United States

passed over: Not promoted at the usual time

PCS: Permanent change of station

petty officer: Noncommissioned officer, seagoing services

PFT: Physical fitness test

PT: Physical training

Ranger: Army infantryman, specially trained in hand-to-hand fighting, surprise raids on enemy posts, scout, and reconnaissance work

recycled: Compelled to repeat part of basic training

remote: An assignment, usually for a year, to a dangerous post, where the military does not send families

ROTC: Reserve Officer Training Corps

SAC: Strategic Air Command

Social Action: Office in charge of EO and drug and alcohol abuse

Specialist: Title indicating expertise in an MOS, followed by a number indicating enlisted rank, as in Spec-4

strike: Get on-the-job training in an MOS

tech school: A school that provides training in an MOS

tender: Ship responsible for maintenance and repair of a Navy combat vessel

TDY: Temporary duty

TI: Training instructor

troop: Enlisted servicemember

watch: Duty, period of responsibility

WAC: Women's Army Corps, dissolved when women were integrated into the service (1978)

WM: Woman Marine

WOPA: Women Officers' Professional Association (seagoing services)

XO: Executive officer